Letts

SUCCESS FOR SCHOOLS

1

KS3 FRAMEWORK COURSE

ICT

INFORMATION & COMMUNICATION TECHNOLOGY

CONTENTS

CONTENTS

UNIT 5 DATA: DESIGNING STRUCTURE, CAPTURING AND PRESENTING

UNIT 6 CONTROL: INPUT, PROCESS AND OUTPUT

UNIT 7 MEASURING PHYSICAL DATA

YOUR NEW SCHOOL'S COMPUTER SYSTEM

AIMS
- To log on to your school's computer system
- To use word-processing software
- To save, retrieve and print your work
- To set up a password

STARTER

Setting the scene
This is the first ICT lesson in your new school.

As a class, spend about 10 minutes making a list of things you used computers for at your last school.
You could also talk about the kind of computer system you had:
- Were the computers linked together?
- What did you have to do before you could start work on the computer?
- Did you need a password?

COMPUTER ROOM RULES

Computers are very expensive.
Your school will have some rules for the use of the computer room, like these two:
- 🖥 Do not eat or drink in the computer room.
- 🖥 Do not bring in your own software to run on the school's computers.

SOFTWARE

The programs that you use on the computer are called <u>software</u>. The programs tell the computer what to do. Your computer system will have many different pieces of software, such as <u>word processing</u> software.

Activity 4

Your teacher will tell you how to start up the word processor on your computer.
- ☐ Type in the rules you are given.
- ☐ Add three or four rules of your own to the list.
- ☐ Type your name at the bottom of the work.
- ☐ Save your work and print it.
- ☐ When you have finished, log off properly.

Activity 3

Make a list of the software that your computer has for you to use.
Explain how you found out.

NETWORKS

A network is a group of computers that are connected together.

A network has lots of advantages:
- You can work from any computer that is on the network.
- You can share very expensive printers.
- Your work can be protected by a password.
- You can access work that has been prepared for you by your teacher.

Activity 1
Write down some other advantages of networks.

LOGGING ON

On a network, the first thing you need to do is to <u>log on</u>. (Your teacher will tell you how to do this.)
When you log on, you are telling the computer who you are.
The computer then knows where to find your work.
When you save your work on a network, it is stored on a computer called a <u>server</u>.

Activity 2
Now try to log on.
If the computer says you cannot log on first time, don't worry. Maybe you did not type something in correctly. Try *one* more time and check that you are typing in *exactly* what you have been told. If you still cannot log on, ask for help.

Log-on

Welcome
Please enter your user name and password

User Name
evans_p_15

Password
••••••••

Enter

REVIEW

5 As a class, spend 5 minutes discussing why passwords are important.
List 3 of the most important reasons.

6 What is the reason for each of the Computer Room rules given on page 4?

7 Why is it important to log off when you have finished?

8 Find out how many computers are connected to your school's system.

9 How many of them can access the Internet?

10 Are they in lots of places around the school? List the rooms where there are computers connected to the network.

STARTING A PRESENTATION

AIMS
- To look at ways of presenting information
- To plan a multimedia presentation
- To use ICT to draft a presentation about yourself

STARTER

⊙⊙ Setting the scene

In this lesson, you are going to start making a multimedia presentation about yourself.

Information is presented in many different ways.

As a class, spend about 10 minutes making a list of different ways that you have seen information presented. Remember – not all the ways will use ICT.

PRESENTING INFORMATION

There are three important things to consider:
- *What* information you are trying to put across?
- *How* are you going to present the information?
- *Who* is the information aimed at?

WHAT?

You are going to make a presentation about yourself on a set of <u>slides</u>.
The slides can be shown on a computer screen or projected
for everyone to see.
You can talk about the slides while they are being shown.
You might want to include this information about yourself:
- *Your hobby*
- *Your favourite music*
- *Your family*
- *Your pets*

Activity 1
Spend 5 minutes writing down some ideas about what information you would like to include.

HOW?

You have lots of choices about how to present your information.
Whatever you decide, computers will make it easy for you.
Your presentation will be a multimedia presentation.
Multimedia means that your work will include more than one of sound, still pictures and moving pictures, as well as written words.
You may be able to display your presentation on a screen with a data projector.

Activity 2

Look at the software available to you on your school's system and decide which is your best choice to let you create a multimedia presentation.
Write down the name of the software and the type of software that it is.
Briefly explain what this software is good at doing.

WHO?

You must think about who will look at your presentation: your audience. You would not use the same approach for a 6-year-old as you would for an adult.

Activity 3

Decide on the audience for your presentation.

DRAFTING AND EDITING

A draft is a first attempt. You need some idea of how much information you have, what the work might look like and an idea of whether it is suited to your audience.
When you have drafted a piece of work, and looked at it, you can then edit it. That means to change it until you are happy with it.

Activity 4

Load the software that you have chosen.
Make a draft of your first page.
Save the page so that you can edit it later.

REVIEW

5 If you were making a presentation for a group of 6-year-olds, what features do you think would be important? Discuss this in a group and then list them.

6 Explain the meanings of these words: audience, draft, edit.

7 List topics that you will use on your other slides.
Collect any information that you will need.

PUTTING YOUR PRESENTATION TOGETHER

AIMS

- To think about how to combine text, images and sound to create an impact
- To include still and moving images, and sound
- To combine text, images and sound to create a multimedia presentation

STARTER

Setting the scene

You have already planned what you are going to do in your presentation. In this lesson, you are going to start putting it together.

As a class, spend about 10 minutes making a list of ideas about how to make a presentation look attractive.

Think about colours, how much to put on each slide and what sort of illustrations you could use.

WHAT'S INCLUDED?

You will be making a 5-minute presentation about yourself to other people, and while showing your slides, you will talk about them.

Your presentation should have 3–5 slides. Make sure each slide is about a different topic, and has a heading.

Your software may have some pre-designed templates. These will help you to start more quickly.

Title

Activity 1 WS 1

You have already drafted one slide.
Write down the main headings that you are going to use for each slide.
Use Worksheet 1 to help you to draft the whole presentation.
Look at your draft and break it down into sections or different topics.

TIPS FOR A GOOD PRESENTATION

- *A presentation should be planned and well-timed. You should plan the slides to be shown and also what you are going to say while they are being shown.*
- *The slides should highlight the main points of what you want to say. You should not just read out what is on the screen.*
- *Movement – called <u>animation</u> – can be used so that each point appears on the screen as you talk about it.*
- *Adding some pictures can be a good idea.*

This slide has a heading, and four points called <u>bullet points</u>.

Activity 2

Suggest a suitable picture to go on this slide.
What else could you do to improve it?

My pets

- 5 rabbits
- 2 cats
- 1 dog
- 2 goldfish

Follow the mouse
http://www.lib.uct.ac.za/infolit/presentation.htm
http://www.presentationbiz.co.uk/articles/articles_hints.htm

SOUND AND MOVEMENT

The bullet points on a slide may be displayed by making them appear one at a time rather than all at once.

There are lots of ways you can make them move on to the slide:

- They can just appear – all together or one at a time.
- They can fly in – from the top, from the bottom or from one side.

> Only use multimedia effects when they are appropriate.

Activity 3

Using Worksheet 1 again, draw on to each slide the direction of movement for the bullet point.

Whatever you decide, have all the points appear in the same way on each slide, so as not to confuse your audience.

Your computer can also make a sound when a point appears. As you will be talking at the time, this may not be a good idea.

REVIEW

4 Look at Slideshow 1. Your teacher will display these for you. In pairs, list (a) what is effective and (b) what is *not* effective about the layout of each slide.

5 Complete the quiz on Worksheet 2.

USING IMAGES AND COLOUR

AIMS
- To discover how colour can make words easier to read
- **To use colour to make a slide look better**
- To discover how pictures can be used to improve a presentation
- To select suitable clip art

STARTER

⊙ Setting the scene

You have already started to develop your presentation. In this lesson, you will use colour and pictures to improve your presentation and to make it more attractive.

Spend 5 minutes on Worksheet 3.
Then compare your answers with other members of your group.

PICTURES

Follow the mouse
http://www.barrysclipart.com
http://school.discovery.com/clipart
http://dgl.microsoft.com

Some people say, 'A picture is worth a thousand words'.
There are lots of sources for pictures:
- A <u>clip art</u> library
- A scanner
- A digital camera
- The Internet

If you use a picture, make sure that it has something to do with your slide.
Ask yourself: 'Does it fit in with what I'm talking about?'

Activity 1

Look at the clip art library that comes with your software.
Choose a picture and put it on one of your slides.

You may need to spend a lot of time searching for the best possible image.
Think about the impression you want to give.
- Serious?
- Humorous?

COLOUR

Colour makes a lot of difference to a presentation. It can make your work much more attractive. You need to be careful though.

Activity 2

Look at the page of this book. Would it look as good in black and white? Look at these two illustrations. Which one looks better?

Can you read this?

Can you read this?

TIPS FOR COLOURS AND SHADES

- *Do not use too many colours on one slide. It looks untidy. Instead, use shades of the same colour.*
- *An important point can be made to stand out by putting it in a different and stronger colour.*
- *Another good idea is to change shades or colours as each bullet point appears. Show the new bullet in a strong colour. At the same time, lighten the other points so they stand out less.*

My pets
- 5 rabbits
- 2 cats
- 1 dog

Activity 3

Load one of your slides. Change the colours of the words.
Try to make the bullet points change as the next one appears.

11

THE FINISHING TOUCHES

AIMS

- To establish rules for using colour
- To look at the use of fonts for headings and text, and those fonts suitable for particular audiences
- To choose a suitable background
- To consider the use of transitions between slides
- To complete the development of your presentation
- To check to see if your presentation is ready

⊙ Setting the scene

Your presentation slides now have colour and pictures. In this lesson, you will link your slides, animate them and put the final touches to your show.

STARTER

Look back at your homework from the last lesson. You wrote some advice for a friend about using colours and pictures in a presentation for young children.

Working as a class, spend about 10 minutes sharing your ideas and making 2 lists:

- The top 5 'things to do' when using colour
- The top 5 'things *not* to do' when using colour

FONTS

The different shapes of letters are called **fonts**.

Fonts can make a difference to the way people respond to your text.

- **Choose a serious font like** Times New Roman **for serious messages.**
- **Use a 'fun' font like** Comic Sans MS **if your presentation is more light-hearted.**

Some fonts are easier to read than others.

USING DIFFERENT FONTS

- **Do not use more than two fonts on one slide.**
- **Use one font for headings and a different one for the text.**
- **Make the headings larger than the text.**
- **Use *italics* and bold with care. It is often better to use colour to make something stand out.**

Activity 2

Look at the font list available for your computer. Try out a few of them.
- ☐ List 5 of the more plain and serious-looking fonts.
- ☐ List 5 fonts that look more light-hearted.

BACKGROUNDS

You need to decide the background for your slides. Giving each slide a different background can confuse your audience. So, it is a good idea to use the same background for *all* your slides.

- For presentations on a computer screen, combine light backgrounds and dark text.
- For presentations using a data projector and screen, choose dark backgrounds and light colour text.

You can have a shaded background, a textured background, or even a picture as the background.

Activity 1

Find out how to change the background on your software. Try some different backgrounds until you find one you like.

Follow the mouse

http://www.isu.edu/itrc/resources/textback/textback.htm

TRANSITIONS AND ANIMATIONS

Your presentation is made from more than one slide. The change between one slide and the next is called a <u>transition</u>.

- Transitions can be sudden, with no movement at all.
- They can use effects like <u>wipe down</u>, where one slide moves down over another.
- With a <u>dissolve effect</u>, one slide blends into the next.

There are many other types of transition. Make sure you do not overdo things. It is best to use the same or similar changes on each slide.

You can arrange for the slides to change after a set time, or change when you click a mouse or press a key. It is most likely that you will want to press a key as you talk.

Activity 3

Use your software to add some transitions to your slides.

CHECKLIST

When your presentation is almost complete, you should check to see if it is ready.

- Is all the text typed in and correct?
- Are the slides in the correct order?
- Have you made good use of colour and background?
- Do your images help to make the points?
- Do your headings stand out?
- Is each slide easy to read (not too full)?
- Have you set the transitions between slides?

Activity 4

Use the checklist to see if your presentation is ready.

REVIEW

5 In pairs, look at each other's presentations. As a group activity, list the most popular transition and animation effects.

6 You will soon be giving your presentation. Complete Worksheet 4. This checklist will help you to think about how you might evaluate your work.

WS 4

13

DELIVERING YOUR PRESENTATION

AIMS
- To prepare to deliver your presentation
- To evaluate your work

⊕ Setting the scene
You have already set up a slide show for your presentation. In this lesson, you will prepare and deliver your presentation.

STARTER

In a group, spend 10 minutes discussing the things you would look for in a good presentation. Think about how it can be made clear and interesting.

NOTES FOR THE SPEAKER

It is a good idea to prepare some notes for what you plan to say in your presentation. These should be easy to read and laid out in the right order. You might want to make a mark in your notes to show where the slides change. Remember, the slides only show the main points you want to make. A good speaker does not just read these points out. The talk should add something to the headings on the slides.

Activity 1
Look at your slides and then write the notes to go with each slide. Remember, your presentation is no more than 5 minutes long.

Notes

My pet is a tabby cat.

She is called Fluffy because she has lots of soft fur.

We got her from a cat rescue centre.

My Pet
- Cat
- Fluffy
- Rescued

Your software may be able to store your notes along with your slides. Use this feature if you can. Otherwise, use a word processor.

GIVING YOUR PRESENTATION

Speaking in front of people is not easy! Here are a few hints:

- *Try to learn what you are going say.*
- *Don't just read your notes. Use your notes only to remind you.*
- *Stand to one side so that everyone can see your slides.*
- *Keep your head up and make regular eye contact with people at the front and at the back of the audience.*
- *Speak up.*

Activity 3

Read through your notes and memorise the main points. You are now ready to give your presentation

EVALUATING A PRESENTATION

When you have finished your presentation, evaluate your performance.

- Could everyone hear you?
- Did you keep to the time?
- Were all your slides clear?
- Did anything go wrong?

You could also ask some of the audience what they thought about it.

Activity 4

Make 2 lists: *What went well* and *What I could have done better.*

NOTES FOR THE AUDIENCE

Often, the audience is given a copy of the slides on a sheet as a reminder of the presentation. The software can print out these handouts for you. Up to ten miniature versions of your slides will fit on one A4 page.

Activity 2

Use your software to make the handouts.

REVIEW

5 As a class, review the process of making a presentation.
- What did you find easy?
- What did you find hard?
- What things could you do better next time?

6 Suppose you were telling someone how to use the same presentation software that you used. Write brief instructions about how to set up the slides and how to create some of the special effects. Write these instructions as a list of bullet points.

SOURCES OF INFORMATION

AIMS
- To look at how to find information
- To look at different sources of information
- To consider who might provide the information for these sources

STARTER

Spend about 10 minutes on this activity. Suppose you, your family or a friend wanted to find out about today's news. As a class, compare the different ways you can find out about the news. Say what are the advantages and disadvantages of each way.

∞ Setting the scene

This is the first in a series of lessons about finding and presenting information.

THE INTERNET

The Internet is one of the places you might go to collect information.

The Internet is a network of thousands of computers across the world. You can probably find information on any topic you would want on the Internet.

The trouble is, there is so much information available that it can be very hard to find exactly what you want.

In addition, information can be put on the Internet by anyone. This means it is not always a reliable source.

By contrast, when you use a book, you could look in the index to help you to find the information you want.

Activity 1

What do you use to find information on the Internet? Make a list of places you often find useful.

CD-ROMS

CD-ROM stands for 'compact disk read-only memory'.

CD-ROMs can also be used to find information. CDs can hold a lot of information. A whole encyclopaedia can fit onto one CD-ROM. Sometimes, they contain information on just one subject, such as science. There is less information to start with, so you are more likely to find what you are looking for. Information on a CD-ROM is usually written by an expert.

Activity 2
Find out how a computer reads the information on a CD-ROM.

BOOKS

Books are a very valuable source of information. Sometimes it is quicker to look for something in a book – assuming you can find the right book! Information in books is normally written by experts in the subject. This can make books a reliable source of information.

Activity 3
Think of some advantages of using books to find things out, compared with using computers.

EMAIL

You might not think of email as a source of information. Have you emailed a friend to ask about homework? If so, you are using email as a source of information.
Some websites have a page where you can send a question in an email to an expert. If you use this method of finding information, you need to be sure that the other person knows something about the subject.

Activity 4
How can you be fairly sure that someone who answers your questions can be relied on?

REVIEW

5 CD-ROMs, email, the Internet, books, television and newspapers can all be used for finding things out. As a class, list the advantages and disadvantages of each method.

6 Choose one of the top news stories of the day. Look at three versions from different sources, such as television, a newspaper, the radio or the Internet. Write some notes on how the sources differ in the way they present the story.

TYPES OF INFORMATION

AIMS

- To look at the types of information available
- **To look at how some information sources are better than others**
- To recognise that some sources are biased
- **To recognise the difference between facts and opinion**

STARTER

In a group, spend about 10 minutes talking about how you have used the Internet to help with a topic or homework you have done recently. Think about how successful you were in finding what you needed.

Setting the scene

You have found some sources of information. This lesson will look at the kind of information you find in those sources and how some sources are better than others.

TYPES OF INFORMATION

Information comes in many different forms:

- Text
- Numbers
- Pictures
- Diagrams
- Video
- Sound

Activity 1

Some sources of information do not contain *all* of these forms of information. Using Worksheet 5, complete the table for the different sources of information.

BIAS

Information is said to be biased if it only looks at one side of the argument. When you collect information from any source you need to be aware that the source might not give a balanced opinion. Some sources may only give one side of the story. In many cases, there may be good reasons for this. You need to try to understand whether you are looking at a balanced picture or not, when you are collecting information for a topic.

Activity 5

Your teacher will give you some website addresses to look at. Do you think any of them show bias?

IS INFORMATION RELIABLE?

Before you use information that you have found, you need to be sure that it is reliable.

Remember that *anyone* can put information on the Internet. So how can you be sure it is accurate? Would you trust a website to diagnose an illness? You need to think about who set up the site, and why it was set up.

If a site is set up by an organisation like the BBC, it is likely to be more reliable than a home website. Even then, you have to make up your own mind.

Activity 2

Working in groups, make a list of some websites that should contain reliable information to help you with school work.

Follow the mouse
http://express.howstuffworks.com

18

FACT OR OPINION?

A **fact** is something that is true. Facts can be proven to be true or they are accepted as true by people who understand the issues.

It is a fact that 2+2=4

An **opinion** is what an individual thinks about something. Different people have different opinions.

It is a matter of opinion whether there are too many cars on the roads. A car dealer might have one opinion and a member of *Friends of the Earth* might have another.

Activity 3

You decide … fact or opinion?
- □ You cannot walk to the Sun.
- □ My teacher is nice.
- □ A library contains books.
- □ Grass is green.
- □ Cars travel too fast past our school.
- □ Saturn has rings.
- □ Organically produced food is better for you.

Activity 4

Use the Internet to find three or four sites where you might find some *facts* about the solar system.

Follow the mouse
http://seds.lpl.arizona.edu/nineplanets/nineplanets/

REVIEW

6 In groups or as a class, spend 5 minutes discussing the websites you have looked at.

7 Complete Worksheet 6.
WS 6

FINDING INFORMATION

AIMS
- **To consider how to find information**
- **To learn about search engines**
- **To find ways of narrowing and widening searches**

STARTER

⊙⊙ *Setting the scene*

You know how to go on the Internet. This lesson concentrates on how to find information that is most useful to you.

Spend about 10 minutes on this activity.
You have probably collected a lot of information in the last week while doing all sorts of schoolwork. Make a list of this information.
For each item, write down where you found it and what type of information it was. If you are not sure about this, take another look at what you did in the last lesson.
Take a look at the range of information everyone collected. What type of information is the most common?

SEARCHING ON THE INTERNET

The Internet gives you access to a huge store of information. The World Wide Web is the part of the Internet that you will look at most of the time. It is a collection of pages that can contain absolutely anything. Anyone can put web pages on the Internet. Often, pages are linked to one another in a website.

There is so much information on the Internet that it is often difficult to find what you need. If you do a search and find a million matches, you cannot possibly read all that you find.

It is easier to find things if you first think about what you really want and then choose your search words carefully.

Activity 1

Suppose you have been asked to do a project on making your home safe for young children.
- Make a list of words you might use in your search.
- Go on to the Internet and try some of the words.
- How useful was the information that you found? Which search words worked best?

SELECT WHAT YOU NEED

How can you pick out what you need from such a vast amount of information? You cannot read every page. Here are some hints.
- **Look at the short summary normally given with the site details.**
- **Look to see if the site has an index page or site map.**
- **Scan the page, looking for important words.**

Activity 3
Complete Worksheet 7.

SEARCH ENGINES

Follow the mouse
Google
Ask Jeeves
Yahoo

A <u>search engine</u> can be used to look things up on the Internet. Search engines are available through websites like Ask Jeeves, Yahoo and Google.

Each search engine has a vast database of keywords and phrases, together with lots of website addresses that mention those key terms. Different search engines produce different results, because they use different methods to find the websites.

Where does the information in a search engine come from?

- When you set up a website, you can decide what key terms are important, and submit them to the search engine companies for inclusion.
- The search engine software scans millions of web pages and then catalogues any terms that seem important.
- Some website owners pay the search engine company to be included as a 'recommended link', for example when you do a search for cheap flights.
- Some search engines also keep track of which websites are the most popular, and place these at the top of the hit list when you do a search.

Activity 2

Carry out this activity with a partner. Choose two different search engines and search using these words.

□ Environment   □ London
□ The Romans   □ Europe

Compare your results.

If you don't find what you need, try another search engine. **❯ go**

BETTER SEARCHING WITH AND/OR

When you find thousands of pages in a search, it can be a good idea to try to reduce the size of the list rather than read all the descriptions.

You can do this by using a <u>complex search</u>. This is where you use more than one search word.

● AND

In Activity 2, you searched for London. If you were looking for information about London buses you could narrow the search down by searching for 'London AND buses'. This will produce fewer results, which will help you to find the information more quickly.

● OR

Sometimes (but not often) a search will produce too few items. When this happens, you need to widen the search. The word **OR** does this.

For example typing 'buses **OR** trains' will find sites with information about either buses or trains.

Activity 4

Try searching for 'London *AND* buses', then compare your result to a search for 'London *OR* buses'. How many hits were there each time? Using your list from Activity 1, see if you can combine the words with *AND* to narrow down your search.

REVIEW

5 As a class, spend 5 minutes discussing the results of Activity 4. Are there any general conclusions you can reach?

6 A friend of yours has not used the Internet before. Write some advice on how to use a search engine.

INTRODUCING THE TOPIC

AIMS
- To consider a particular topic: genetically modified (GM) food
- To judge whether a website presents facts or opinions

STARTER

Spend about 10 minutes on this activity.
Here are answers to some questions:
- *Biased*
- *Narrow down*
- *www*
- *Key word*
- *Google*

For each answer, work out the question that gives that answer and write it down.
Now, look at what others have done and compare your questions.

⊙⊙ Setting the scene

This is the first lesson on a new topic: GM food. In the next few lessons, you will collect information on this topic and prepare a presentation that gives a balanced view of the issues.

THE TOPIC

Many people are arguing about GM food. Some people think it should be allowed. Others want it banned. It is a topic that provokes strong opinions.

You are going to put together a presentation that gives *both* sides of the argument. You are not trying to persuade, so you must try to keep *your* views out of it.

You will need to use a presentation package, and you should also prepare some background material in the form of handouts to go with it. The background material should also be balanced.

Activity 1

Visit the websites listed in the 'Follow the mouse' box. Do they give a balanced view? Write down what you think.

Follow the mouse
http://www.newscientist.com/hottopics/gm/
http://www.scope.educ.washington.edu/gmfood/
http://reason.com/bi/bi-gmf.shtml

WARNING

GM CROP FIELD TRIAL

A GOOD PRESENTATION

Try to make your presentation as professional as you can. Here are some suggestions:

- Keep it balanced.
- Make the slides simple and clear.
- Make sure the text is big enough to read from the back of the room.
- Do detailed research.
- Write a script.

Activity 2

The last time you did a presentation, you *reviewed* it. Look at that review again. Add three more suggestions for making good presentations, based on your own experience.

FACT OR OPINION?

Since this topic involves many people with different and quite opposite views you will need to select the information you use carefully. It is unlikely you will find one place giving a balanced view. Some of the information will be clearly biased. It can sometimes be difficult to decide what is opinion and what is fact.

Activity 3 WS 8

Complete Worksheet 8.

IT'S ALL IN THE ADDRESS

Sometimes, you know exactly where to find information. You then type in the address of the web page that you want.

Every web page has its own address. It is called a <u>URL</u>. URL stands for uniform resource locator.

Address: http://www.bbc.co.uk > go

For example, www.bbc.co.uk is the URL of the BBC. This URL leads to all their other pages. Is information here likely to be trustworthy?

www.Becci.sunridge.pinkcity.com looks like it might belong to someone called Becci. Does this make you think differently about what you find there?

The last part of the address gives some clues.

- .com *probably means a company –* somewhere in the world, maybe in the USA.
- .co.uk *probably means a company in the UK.*
- .org.uk *means an organisation based in the UK, but do you know what sort of an organisation?*
- .gov.uk *means the government in the UK. Does that make it trustworthy?*

Activity 4

What do think these stand for?

- ☐ ac.uk
- ☐ sch.uk
- ☐ co.de
- ☐ biz
- ☐ me.uk

REVIEW

5 As a class, suggest search words that you could use in an Internet search for suitable information about GM food.

6 Your presentation will need about 6 slides. Make a draft plan of what will go on each slide.

23

COLLECTING INFORMATION

AIMS
- To look at collecting information for use in your presentation
- To plan your research
- To analyse material
- **To learn how to use bookmarks**

STARTER

WS 9

Spend about 10 minutes completing the word search on Worksheet 9.

⚭ *Setting the scene*
Your skills in searching the World Wide Web for information
will now be used to find information about the topic of GM food. In this lesson, you will plan your research and

PLANNING RESEARCH

The issue of GM food has attracted a lot of attention. Therefore, you will find a lot of information on the web about it.
It is important that you go about your research in a planned way. Otherwise, you may spend a long time but find nothing useful.

Activity 2
Look at the plan for your presentation. For each slide, write down which viewpoint you need for that slide, for or against.

- To be balanced, you need more than one viewpoint. Try to find some sites in favour and some against.
- Plan your search words. If you are finding lots of hits, then think about how to narrow down the search.
- Set yourself a time limit to find your material.

Load browser
→
Go to search engine
→
Enter search words
→
Too many hits?
Yes → Use AND
No
→
Read summary
→
Follow useful link

BOOKMARKS

A <u>bookmark</u> is a quick way of remembering the web address of a page you have found useful. Bookmarks are sometimes called <u>favourites</u>.

When you are searching for information, you will look at many sites. You should skim over a page very quickly to see if it may help you. If it is no use, leave it quickly and try another. If it looks as if it might be useful, bookmark the page. (Your software might call this <u>adding to favourites</u>.)

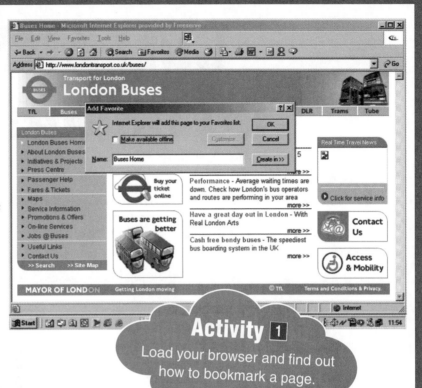

Activity 1

Load your browser and find out how to bookmark a page.

ANALYSING MATERIAL

When you find a site, skim the first page and try to answer these questions:
- What is the purpose of the site?
- Who is it aimed at?
- What is its viewpoint?
- Has it any images that I can use?
- Has it any text that I can use?

Activity 3

Visit four sites, and write down the URL for each.
Answer these questions for each site.
- Is the site in favour of GM food or against it? Maybe it considers both sides.
- Who, or what organisation wrote it?
- Who is supposed to be influenced by this site?

Then decide if it is likely to be helpful to you. Remember that a web page can be very long and if you print it, this could waste a lot of paper. So, only print the parts you actually need. Better still, copy and paste them into your work.

REVIEW

4 In small groups, spend 5 minutes brainstorming your ideas for your presentation. Write down your main points.

5 Planning your research is very important. Because of this, you have 3 lessons to prepare your presentation and the information sheets to go with it. Produce a plan showing your targets for the next 3 lessons.

COLLATING INFORMATION

AIMS

- To look at what can be done with information that has been collected
- To look at how to lay out your presentation
- To find out how to collect information into a document
- To consider copyright issues

STARTER

Spend about 10 minutes on this activity.
- Complete Worksheet 10.
- In small groups, discuss your findings.

⚭ Setting the scene
In this lesson, you will collate the information you have collected so far, and plan your presentation.

This product may contain genetically modified produce.

5 018374 064

COPYRIGHT

If you see this symbol, ©, or the word '<u>copyright</u>' on anything, it means the work should *not* be copied. It says the work belongs to the person who wrote it.
Look inside the back of this book. Can you find the © symbol?

Internet sites often do not put copyright on them, but the information still belongs to the person who created it, even if this is not the person who set up the site.
It is still someone's work and you should not try to pretend that it is your own.

<u>Plagiarism</u> is copying someone's work and then saying that you did the work yourself.
If you do use information that someone else produced, then you should say where it comes from and to whom it belongs.
This is called *acknowledging the source*.
You should *always* acknowledge the source of your information.

Activity 1

Look at the BBC website: www.bbc.co.uk
Can you find the © symbol on the first page?
Follow the link that goes with it. It gives a lot of legal information about the copyright of the BBC's pages.

YOUR PRESENTATION

How much of the information that you have collected are you going to use?

Your presentation will be better if it is divided into sections:

● Introduction

> Today, I am going to talk about …

● The case for

> Some people think that …

● The case against

> Other people disagree. They say that …

● Summing up

> So, looking at the whole topic …

● Acknowledgements

Activity 2

Look at the information you have collected, and highlight the parts that will be used.

You could do this by printing it out, or by changing the text colours in the word processor.

TIPS

● Keep your introduction brief.
● Spend about the same time on each side of the argument.
● Don't include too much detailed information.
● Try to be fair to each side of the argument.

It's a presentation

COPYING AND PASTING

You should already know how to copy and paste text and pictures. You can use this technique to gather information that you need for use in the future.

If you open a word-processing document, and also the Internet browser, you can copy and paste material from web pages straight into your document. You will then build up a document with all the material that may be of use. Remember to write down where it all came from.

Activity 3

Load your word processor and an Internet page. Practise copying and pasting text from the web page to your document.

REVIEW

4 In pairs, discuss why individuals and organisations need to copyright their work. As a group, list the most important reasons.

5 You need to collect some information for a fact sheet on genetically modified food. Complete Worksheet 11.

PUTTING IT ALL TOGETHER

AIMS
- To produce a slide presentation putting forward a balanced view of the topic

STARTER

As a class, spend about 10 minutes writing a list of special effects that can make a presentation as effective as possible.

⊙⊙ Setting the scene
You should have all the information you need. In this lesson, you will write the presentation slides and the notes to go with them.

HOW TO USE PRESENTATION SOFTWARE

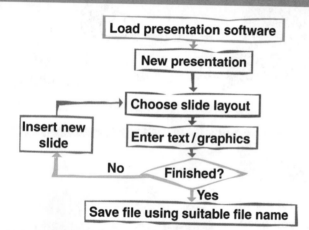

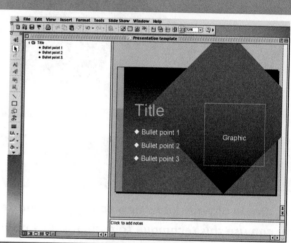

THE INTRODUCTION

In the introduction, you should catch the audience's attention and make them want to hear more. Otherwise, you could put them off completely.

You only need one slide for your introduction. Use it like a headline and very briefly outline what your presentation is about. A well-chosen graphic could help.

Activity 1
Bullet points are good for an introduction. Load your presentation software and make a slide with 4–5 points for your introduction.

THE BODY

You need 4 slides for this section:
- 2 slides could argue for GM foods
- 2 slides could argue against GM foods.

For
- greater yield per acre of land
- less need to use harmful chemicals
- medicines could be grown in crops

Against
- possible long-term health dangers
- natural crops may be contaminated
- mutation of plants and animals

Look at the information you have gathered and pick out about 4 points for each slide.
Try to separate facts from opinions.

Activity 2
Set up your slides to present the case for and the case against. It is up to you to decide which comes first.

THE CONCLUSION

Your presentation should end with one final slide:
- Sum up what you have said.
- Be brief – one slide is enough.
- Include the main points that you have already made.

GM FOODS
Class 7B decides ...

Activity 3
As before, use bullet points.
Make a slide with 4–5 bullet points for your conclusion. Make sure it is a little different from your introduction, though.

Activity 4
Make one final slide, listing the sources of information:
- The author
- The name of the website
- The date the material was written

SOURCES

Remember to acknowledge the sources of your information.

REVIEW

5 As a class, spend 5 minutes defining these words: biased, viewpoint, fact, opinion, copyright.

6 Before you make your presentation, you will need some notes to go with it. Use Worksheet 12 to help you to prepare your notes.

WS 12

PRODUCING HANDOUTS

AIMS
- To make a handout to add further information to your presentation
- **To look at what needs to go into the handout**
- To find out how to edit and select text

STARTER

In small groups, spend about 10 minutes having a brainstorming session to come up with a list of ten words that you associate with word processing, such as margins and fonts.
As a class, collect some of these words together and check that you know what they all mean.

◯◯ Setting the scene
Your presentation is almost complete and in this lesson, you will make a handout to add further information.

EDITING TEXT

You may need to arrange all the background material in a better order.
To select text, move the mouse over the bit you want while holding down the mouse button.

Activity 2
Load your document and highlight some text using the mouse. Can you drag the text about? Now try using the keys alone to do the same thing.

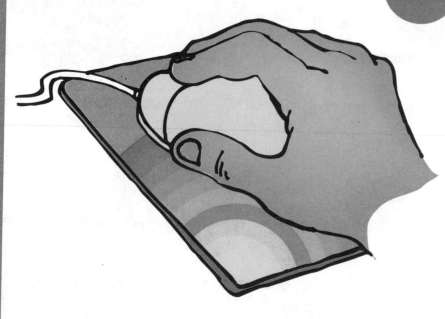

Clicking twice will select a word.

Clicking three times will select a whole paragraph.

You can also select text using the shift key and the cursor keys. This is often easier than using the mouse.

Once you have selected some text, you can paste it somewhere else in the document or delete it.
- *To delete highlighted text, just press the <u>delete</u> key.*
- *To move some text, you can use <u>cut</u> and <u>paste</u>. Or, with practice, you can use the mouse to <u>drag and drop</u> it to where you want it. Which is easier?*

WHAT'S IN THE HANDOUT?

As well as the presentation you will give, you also need to put together some background information to give to your audience.

- Just printing your presentation is not enough.
- You need no more than 2 pages.
- Some information that you provide should *not* be in your presentation.
- Use material collected from various sources.

Remember to acknowledge your sources!

Activity 1

Look at the information you have bookmarked previously.
Can you use any of this? If so, copy and paste it into your handout.

THE PROFESSIONAL LOOK

The material you have pasted into your sheet will be from a variety of places. It may be in different fonts, colours and sizes.

If it is, it will not look good, and so you need to improve it. It will look better if it is all in the same font. You can do this very quickly by selecting the whole document and then choosing a particular font and size of text. This is a formal document. So it should be a plain font such as Times Roman, and in a size that is easy to read. Most formal documents are printed in 10 point or 12 point.

Activity 3

Load the document. Select it all. Can you find a way of doing this in one go?
Change the font and size to make the text look formal.
Check to see that it is all in one colour.

Times Roman

REVIEW

4 Look at the results of the brainstorming you did at the start of this lesson.
How many of the features that came up in the word list have you used?

5 In the next lesson, you will be giving your presentation.
Use Worksheet 13 to help you to prepare.

PRESENT AND EVALUATE

AIMS

- To identify the purpose of the presentation
- To consider using prompt cards
- To make your presentation
- To evaluate the presentation

PROMPT CARDS

A successful presentation requires more than just reading from a piece of paper. This can be very boring. If you can, memorise more or less what you are going to say. Many people find this difficult and need some notes.

A good way is to use prompt cards – some pieces of card about postcard size, one for each slide. Write down a few words or phrases that will remind you what to say. Try not to write too much or you will just read it!

Activity 3

Read the text in this panel, then write down some key points that you could use to remember what is in it.

PURPOSE

Presentations can be used for a variety of purposes:

- Communicating information to the audience
- Persuading the audience to see your point of view
- Demonstrating something

The purpose of this presentation is to communicate information to the audience about GM foods.

Activity 2

Look over your presentation and think about each slide. Does it give the audience any information? If it does not, then maybe you need to improve it!

EVALUATION

When you have given your presentation, you should evaluate how things went:

- What did you do well?
- What did not go so well?
- Did the audience ask any questions? What sort of questions?
- Did the slides look OK? Were they clear?
- Ask a few of your friends what they thought!

Activity 4

Use Worksheet 15 to help you with the evaluation.

STARTER

Complete the word search on presentation techniques on Worksheet 14.

⦾ Setting the scene
In this final lesson in this unit, you will present your findings to your class, and evaluate your performance and that of others in your class.

TIPS FOR PRESENTING

- Make the slides simple. Do not overdo the colour.

My pets
- 5 rabbits
- 2 cats
- 1 dog
- 2 goldfish

My pets
- 5 rabbits
- 2 cats
- 1 dog
- 2 goldfish

- Check the order and the animations beforehand.
- Be prepared – read your information sheet.
- Check that you can load your file.
- Give an introduction.

Hello!

- Be ready to answer any questions afterwards.

Activity 1
Make a list of some of the different animation effects that you can do with your software.

REVIEW

5 As a class, spend 5 minutes sharing the good points of each other's presentations and talking about what might be improved.

6 What are short cut keys?

7 Write down 2 features of a presentation package.

8 What is a search engine?

9 Which word narrows down a search?

10 What does URL stand for? What might the URL tell you?

INTRODUCING THE TOPIC

AIMS
- Introduction to the topic: a booklet about your town
- To agree methods of working for your group

STARTER

As a class, spend about 5 minutes listing the things that a word processor can do. Then spend about 5 minutes more suggesting where you might use these features.

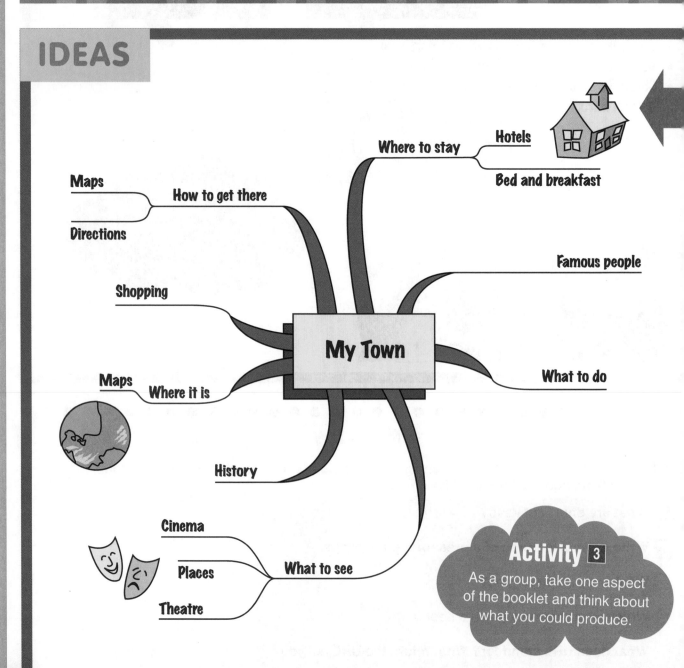

⬭ *Setting the scene*

This lesson is the start of a new unit, and you will be introduced to your new topic: a booklet about your town.

IDEAS

Where to stay — Hotels
Bed and breakfast

Maps — How to get there
Directions

Famous people

Shopping

Maps — Where it is

My Town

What to do

History

Cinema

Places — What to see

Theatre

Activity 3
As a group, take one aspect of the booklet and think about what you could produce.

THE TOPIC

Your group will be working together to produce a booklet about your town for visitors. Depending on where you live, you may want to consider a city or a village.

The idea is to make an information booklet and to collect together, in one document, these features:

● Photographs ● Drawings ● Text

Activity 1
Consider the audience for this booklet: who might they be and what might they be looking for?

WORKING TOGETHER

One of the skills you will develop in this unit is how to work together.

You will be working in groups to produce the booklet. Each of you will need to contribute about 2 pages.

The booklet must have images and text from various sources. The content must be up-to-date and relevant.

Activity 2
Spend a few minutes organising your group. You might like to think about these things.
☐ Where is the information coming from?
☐ Who will collect the information?
☐ Who will co-ordinate the group?

Follow the mouse
http://www.cam.ac.uk/cambuniv/style/
http://www.abs.aston.ac.uk/guide.html

SHARE IT OUT

There will be lots of ideas for the booklet. You are not all going to be able to do everything.

You will need to decide how many pages to include in the booklet and who in your group will produce which page. So that it all looks much the same, you will need to agree a common format for the booklet. This is called <u>house style</u>. It should cover things like these:
● **The fonts used**
● **The margin sizes**
● **The size of fonts**
● **The names used to save the work**

Activity 4
In your group, discuss and agree the house style, the topics each of you will work on and the amount of page space each of you will produce.

- -

REVIEW

5 As a class, spend 5 minutes discussing where you could collect information from for your booklet. Write down any good ideas that others suggest.

6 Collect a newspaper page and some leaflets with any kind of information about your town. Bring them to the next lesson.

PAGE LAYOUT AND DESIGN

AIMS
- To look at page layout and design
- To learn about use of colour, text layout and frames

STARTER

List as many computer bits and pieces as you can in 5 minutes.

As a class, compare lists. What was the most common item?

∞ Setting the scene

This lesson is the first of several in which you will produce a booklet, using desktop publishing software, and working in small groups together.

BASIC PAGE LAYOUT

A page is made up of a set of frames. Each can be moved about on its own until you are happy with the page layout. This drawing shows a page with a number of frames.

Frame for headline

Picture frame

Frames for text

Activity 4

Load your desktop publishing (DTP) software and set up some frames in the same pattern as the drawing in this panel.

NEWSPAPERS

Look at the newspaper pages that people have brought in. You should see that, in some ways, the pages are laid out in the same way:

- Each article has a <u>headline</u> to attract your attention.
- Its font is different from the rest of the article.
- The paper is arranged in <u>columns</u>.
- Some text fits around pictures.
- Some pictures are in boxes to make them stand out.

Activity 1

Take a page from a newspaper.
Label these features:
- ☐ A column
- ☐ A headline
- ☐ A sub heading
- ☐ Some bold text
- ☐ Some body text

LEAFLETS

Many of the other leaflets that have been brought in will be in colour. This makes them look more attractive. You are more likely to look at a colour leaflet than one in just black and white.

Colour is used in this book to make it look good and easier to follow.

Activity 2

Look at some of the leaflets that have been brought in. Choose one and write a short paragraph, describing the features that attract your attention.

TEXT LAYOUT

There are 4 ways of laying out text on the page.

A piece of text can be set up so that all the lines line up on the left. This is **aligned left**.

A piece of text can be set up so that all the lines line up on the right. This is **aligned right**.

A piece of text can be set up so that all the lines line up in the middle. This is **centred**.

A piece of text can be set up so that all the lines line up on both sides. This is **fully justified**.

The way text is aligned is called <u>justification</u>. Notice how the computer adds spaces between words, to line up both margins in the <u>fully justified</u> example.

Activity 3

Load a document you have produced before. Any document will do. Use the formatting commands to try out the 4 different layouts.

REVIEW

5 Look carefully at this page. Discuss how colour, headings, sub-headings and frames have been used to make the page easy to follow.

6 Take a page from a newspaper, and use a pen to draw on it where the frames might be. (Make sure no one wants the page first!)

GRAPHIC CAPTURE METHODS

AIMS

- **To build on work already done on combining text and graphics**
- **To identify image requirements**
- To capture still and moving images using a variety of ICT tools
- **To choose the most appropriate method of acquiring and processing images**

STARTER

Where do the images on websites, or in magazines, newspapers and books come from? As a class, spend 10 minutes making a spider diagram on the whiteboard showing everything you know about images.

∞ Setting the scene

You already know how to layout a page to include text and graphics. In this lesson, you will select and capture the graphics to support your text.

Follow the mouse

www.bapla.org
http://www.clipart.com/
http://www.vnunet.com/Products/Hardware/Scanner

IMAGES

The booklet you have been working on will need images to make it attractive. Here are some of the ways you might obtain images:

- Scanning pictures
- Taking photos on a digital camera
- Downloading images from the web
- Using clip art

Activity 1

Decide on at least 4 images you will need for your booklet. For each one, say how you will make the image ready for use in the computer.

DIGITAL CAMERAS

Digital cameras come in many shapes and sizes. They are now very widely used. Instead of using film, they store photos as numbers that a computer can use. The camera has a sensor called a **CCD** that converts light into electrical charges. These are converted into images by the camera. You can then transfer your images to a computer and use them in a document.

Activity 3

Import *Image 1* provided into your DTP package. Resize it so that it fits on the page. Practise changing the size of the image and moving it around the page.

STORAGE

Compression reduces the amount of space needed for storage. JPEGs (Joint Photographic Experts Group) are a way of storing high-quality colour and black and white photographs in bitmap form.

Activity 5

The two images – *Image 2* and *Image 3* – are the same image. One is saved as a JPEG, the other is a bitmap.
- Use *Windows Explorer* or *My Computer* to look at the storage space needed for these two image files. Which one takes up more space?
- Import them both into your DTP software and resize them. Which is best to work with? Why?

SCANNERS

Scanners come in many shapes and sizes, but they all do much the same job. They allow you to take a photograph or drawing on paper and transfer it to the computer.

- **Flatbed scanners** usually have a flat glass plate over a moving scanner head and a cover over the glass. You can put documents or photographs on top of the glass. A light under the glass shines on the page being scanned and is picked up by the scanner head.

- A **hand-held scanner** is only 1–13 centimetres wide, making it portable. It plugs into your computer, so it is also easy to share. Sometimes, it is used with a laptop computer. If you use a handheld scanner for a whole A4 document, you have to go over it in strips. The software then tries to match up the strips.

- People in the graphics or publishing industry use **film and slide scanners** for very high quality images. Slides and film are very small, so the scanner needs to have a very **high resolution** so that, when the image is made bigger, it still looks good. The quality of a resolution is measured by the number of dots per square inch (**dpi**) used to produce images in printing or on a computer screen.

> **Activity** WS 16
> Complete Worksheet 16.

WHAT IS A DIGITAL IMAGE?

> **Activity** 4 WS 17
> Complete Worksheet 17.

Digital images are made up from many tiny dots called **pixels**. Your computer and printer use these pixels to display or print photographs. The more pixels there are, the better the image will look. The more pixels the display uses, the more memory is needed to store the image. This table shows the resolution needed for different sizes of photograph.

Print size	Image resolution
Wallet (2 × 3 inches)	640 × 480 pixels
10.16 cm × 12.70 cm (4 × 5 inches)	768 × 512 pixels
12.70 cm × 17.78 cm (5 × 7 inches)	1152 × 768 pixels
20.32 cm × 25.40 cm (8 × 10 inches)	1536 × 1024 pixels

- -

REVIEW

6 Quick-fire quiz.
In groups, take 5 minutes to prepare brief answers to these 3 questions. Your teacher will write down 3 answers to each question and ask the class to discuss which is the best and why.

- What is a pixel?
- Why do film scanners need to be very high resolution?
- Why is compression sometimes used to store image files?

7 As a class, look again at your spider diagram. What changes would you like to make to it? These could take the form of additions, corrections or deletions.

8 You will need to collect some images for your booklet:
- Well-known buildings in your town
- Places of interest
- Some old photographs or postcards of places

GRAPHICS PACKAGES

AIMS
• To learn about different ways of creating and editing images

STARTER

 WS 18

Complete the crossword on Worksheet 18.

⬤⬤ Setting the scene
In the last lesson, you found some images to include in your booklet. In this lesson, you will learn how to edit these images.

TYPES OF GRAPHIC SOFTWARE

There are two different ways of storing images and graphics on a computer:
● Vector graphics
● Bitmap graphics

The way you choose depends on the image and how you intend to use it.

Vector graphics can be scaled to larger and smaller sizes without distorting the image or losing clarity. They do not need much storage space.
Bitmap images can be scaled but they can become distorted if made too big. They use a lot of storage space.

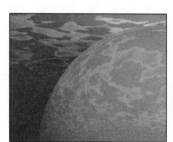

 **Activity 1**

Load your DTP software. Import the two images called *Image 2* and *Image 3*. Try changing the size of each image. Watch what happens to them. Which one is the bitmap image?

REVIEW

5 As a class, spend 5 minutes discussing the different features of the packages.

6 Produce a table to compare the different features of graphic packages you have looked at in this lesson.

DRAWING PACKAGES

Drawing packages produce vector type images – images made from objects and shapes. You can change the size and position of each object separately to change the final image.

Activity 2

Load your drawing package and make this simple image.

Try moving parts of the image around. See how easy it is!

PAINTING PACKAGES

Painting packages produce bitmapped images. These are more difficult to work with. Once you have drawn something, you cannot easily move it about – it is not an object but a collection of pixels.

The package will have some tools to help you to edit the image.

Activity 3

Load your painting package and try to make the same image as before. Then try to make changes to it. How do the two ways of editing compare?

PHOTOGRAPHIC PACKAGES

Although photographs are bitmaps and can be handled by a painting package, most scanners and digital cameras have special software for photographs. They allow you to work with photographs and to alter things like contrast and brightness. You can sometimes improve the look of a photograph using these tools.

 ## Activity 4

Load *Image 4* and *Image 5*. These are the same photograph with the contrast and brightness changed.

DESKTOP PUBLISHING

AIMS
- To look at desktop publishing
- To find out what DTP is
- To learn about page layout, re-sizing and moving objects

⊙⊙ Setting the scene
This lesson builds on your DTP skills.

STARTER

Spend about 5 minutes writing down as many words as you can think of that are to do with page layout.
Spend a little time making a class list.
Are there any words on your list that are *not* layout words?

WHAT IS DTP?

Desktop publishing (DTP) is using a computer to set out a page. It is done with DTP software, which can handle images and text. DTP software is not usually used for typing documents.

The words in the document are called **text**. To prepare the text, a word processor is used. The text is saved to a file and then set in place in the final document using the DTP software.

Images can be drawings, diagrams or photographs. They will be prepared using software designed for the kind of image needed.

Activity 1
Load your DTP software and look at the tools available for page layout.

Try holding the mouse cursor over some of the buttons and looking at the tool tips.

OBJECTS

Each page is laid out as a series of objects, or frames. Each object is treated as a separate item that can easily be re-sized, moved or deleted. Each object, when selected, will have markers called <u>handles</u> around its frame. These are used to alter its size.

Activity 2
Load your DTP software and practise re-sizing some objects.

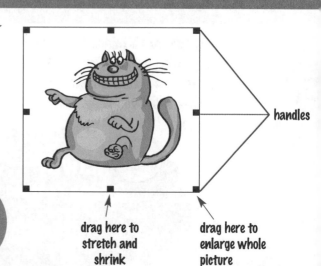

handles

drag here to stretch and shrink

drag here to enlarge whole picture

LAYOUT

The DTP package is used to design the page layout:

- Text boxes are set up to hold the text.
- Frames are put in place to hold the images.

The DTP software allows the images to be resized:

- The text can be made to fit round the images.
- Columns can be set up and joined together so that the words flow from the bottom of one column to the top of the other.

Once the layout has been designed, the text from the word processor is <u>imported</u> and flowed in. The pictures are also imported. This produces the final page. The images and the text can be moved about until the page is looking the way it should.

Activity 3 **WS 19**

Use Worksheet 19 to help you to produce a page that looks like this.

LOCAL NEWS

Special points of interest:

New Industrial Park

- 55 acres
- Predicted 250 trees will have to be cut down for the park to be built.
- The estate will have 23 units.
- Employment for 100 people
- 2 farms lost

One of the farms

New Industrial Park

News from the Enterprise Company is that they are hoping to build a new Industrial Park in the village of Romsley. A spokesman for the company said:

"We might as well do something with the land. All it's used for is farming, and there's an old farm house which hasn't been used in donkey's years! It's also near a busy road and not too far from Birmingham Airport."

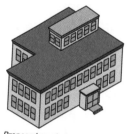

Proposed new industrial unit

Mrs. Clean from the village gave her views on this Industrial Park. She commented:

"Think about this. You're going out for a walk through the countryside and you're looking at all the wonderful flowers and animals when you see this big massive great building. It will totally wreck the view. The amount of pollution that they will be giving off will be horrific. There will be extra noise from traffic. We're all against it."

Your Views

The owner of the farm said, "It's my farm and I can do what I want with my land."

We spoke to Mrs. Shultz, also from the village. She said: "I think it's a great idea. There would be more business in the area. There is plenty of space available, good roads and the area needs employment. I will apply for a job when it comes in."

87% of the people that we interviewed said that they would like to keep Romsley how it is. The other 13% wanted an Industrial Park in Romsley.

REVIEW

4 As a class activity, list the features found in a DTP package that are *not* found in a word-processing package.

5 Choose 3 features of a DTP package and write a description of them – what they do and how you use them.

PLANNING

AIMS
- To start planning a DTP project
- To learn about structure diagrams and sequencing events

STARTER

 WS 20 Spend about 5 minutes with a partner using Worksheet 20.

⚭ Setting the scene
In this lesson, you will plan how to use your DTP skills to produce your booklet.

PLANNING STEP BY STEP

Most big jobs can be broken down into smaller ones. This makes it easier to do and you make fewer mistakes. Once you have worked out what the small jobs are, you can put them into order and start work on them.

It is important to order these little jobs correctly. For example, a builder cannot put the roof on a house until he has built the walls.

In the same way, you cannot put a photograph on a page until someone has taken it, captured it, and saved it on the computer.

Activity 1
Write down the steps needed to load your DTP package. When you have done this, compare the steps you wrote with those of one of your friends.

TIME-SCALE

Your team now knows what needs to be done and the order to do it in.

Since each member of the team needs something to do you need to agree who does what and when.

Remember that some tasks cannot be done before others are finished.

Activity 4
Agree the dates by which each person will have their contribution ready.

PLANNING TOGETHER

Putting the booklet together as a team will need planning. The better the planning, the easier the job will be, and the better you will work together.
If one member of the team is producing photographs, the photographs must be ready and saved on the computer for the person doing the layout.

Activity 2
Make a list of jobs that need doing to put your booklet together. Do not worry too much about the order yet.

STRUCTURE DIAGRAMS

When a large task like yours needs to be done it is often better to break it down in the form of a diagram.
One way to do this is to use the **top-down method**. This starts with the big task at the top. It is then broken down into smaller tasks at the bottom.
This example of a structure diagram is based on your GM foods presentation.

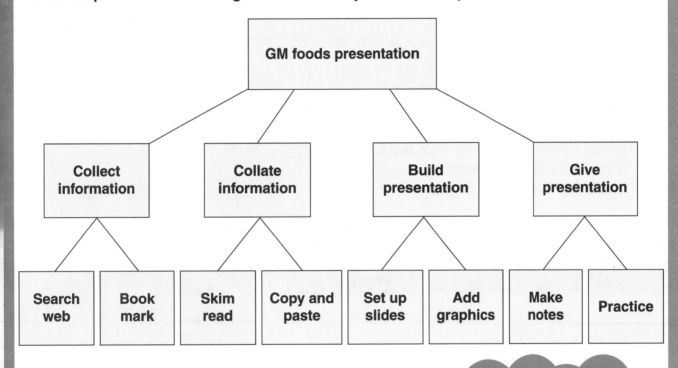

Different people may produce different diagrams for the same task, it depends on how they each see the task broken down.

Activity 3
Take the list of steps from Activity 2 and make a structure diagram from them.

REVIEW

5 As a class, spend 5 minutes sharing your list of tasks. Make a list of common tasks.

6 Produce a sketch plan of one page from your booklet.

DIRECTIONS

AIMS
- **To look at producing a map as part of a booklet**
- **To consider different ways of making the map**

STARTER

These words are answers to some questions:
- Frame
- Template
- House style
- DTP
- Colour
- Graphic

Spend 5 minutes making up some questions, which lead to these answers.

Then, spend another 5 minutes comparing your questions with other people in the class.

◌◌ Setting the scene

This is the first of five lessons in which you will develop your booklet. During these 5 lessons, your group will produce a map, details of interesting places to visit, where visitors might stay, shopping facilities and some history of your town or village.

MAKING MAPS

Perhaps the best way of giving directions is to use a map.
Here are some suggestions for producing maps:
- You could draw one on paper and then scan it.
- You could draw one on the computer.
- You could try to find one on the Internet.

Activity 2
Go to www.multimap.com
Enter the name of your town or a postcode.
Remember that, if use these maps, you must acknowledge your source.

MORE ABOUT IMAGES

If you do use a map, it may be helpful to include some written directions too.

Remember that the map is an **image**, whichever way you produce it.

There are several ways you can combine images with text.

Activity 3
Load your DTP package and try out some different text wrapping techniques.

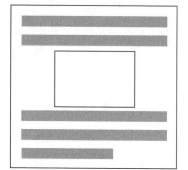

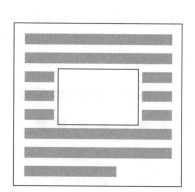

The way they combine is called **text wrap**.

HOW TO GET THERE

If people are coming to your town they need to know where it is. You will probably give directions in different ways to different people. How you give directions depends on where they live:

● Is it for people who live far away?
● Is it for people who live nearby?

- Join M5 at junction 20 (northbound).
- Follow M5 to J3.
- Leave J3 and take A456 signposted to Birmingham.

- Follow the High Street past the Land Oak pub.
- Turn right at traffic lights.
- Go past supermarket on left.
- Take next left into Willow Road.

Activity 1

Think about your booklet. What difference does it make to the directions if people come from far away?

SOFTWARE

If you decide to draw your own map, there are two types of software you could use:

● Bitmap software
● Vector graphics software

You could use either type of software to trace over a map downloaded from the Internet.

Activity 4

Choose the best method for your map and give reasons for your choice.

REVIEW

5 As a class, spend 5 minutes discussing who the map in your booklet is aimed at and how your group might produce a map.

6 Make a table showing the advantages and disadvantages of the different ways of producing a map.

WHAT TO SEE IN MY TOWN

AIMS
- To look at some of the material that will be in a booklet
- To consider meeting the needs of your audience

STARTER

As a class, spend about 5 minutes discussing some of the places you can go to in your town or village.

⚭ Setting the scene
In this lesson, work on the booklet continues.

USING FRAMES

Each page of your booklet is made up of frames.
Here are some of the things you can do with frames.

Activity 3
Load your DTP package and try out some of these effects.

Put a picture behind the text to create a watermark effect

← Make columns →

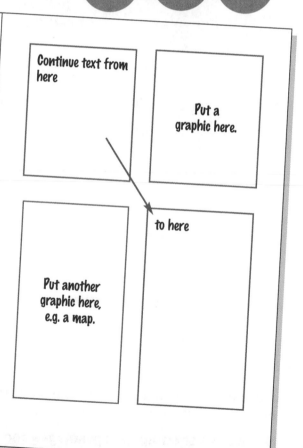

Continue text from here

Put a graphic here.

to here

Put another graphic here, e.g. a map.

AUDIENCE

Look at the class list of ideas about places to go. Are *all* the places you thought of interesting to everyone?

Younger people generally have different interests to older people. They want to see and do different things.

Your booklet needs to be designed to appeal to everyone.

You could do this by having separate sections in the booklet, or by making sure that the list is well balanced. You could do some research by asking people of different ages what they are interested in when they visit a new town.

Activity 1

You need to decide how your booklet is going to cater for all age groups. How are you going to set out your pages to deal with this?

ADVERTS

Advertising is often used to help to sell booklets of this type.

Adverts are often priced according to how much space they take up. They need to achieve the maximum impact in the space allowed.

So, they need to be eye-catching.

Activity 2

Your school is to hold a summer fair and wants to place an advert in your booklet. The school has paid for a space, which is 6 cm by 4 cm.
Write an advertisement that will fit into this space.

Putting a **box** around an advert can make it **stand out.**

REVIEW

4 Spend 5 minutes with another group looking at their advertisement.

5 As a class activity, spend 5 minutes discussing what makes a good advert.

6 Using no more than 100 words, describe a DTP package to someone who has not used one before.

MORE ABOUT CONTENT

AIMS
- To continue adding information on where to stay
- To look at points of good design
- To share work

STARTER

As a class, discuss the audience for the booklet. You should look at the needs of different groups of people.

⬭ Setting the scene
In this lesson, you continue adding information to the booklet and start thinking about the design of the booklet.

WHERE TO STAY

This section of your booklet should provide information about places to stay in your town. You will need to collect some information on places to stay.

Here are some possible sources of information:
- The local tourist information office
- The Internet
- Local library
- Newspaper adverts

You need to consider how to present this information in an accessible way. One way may be to set up a table.

Activity 1
Look at your DTP package. Can you set up a table easily? What information would someone want about where to stay?

SHARING YOUR WORK

You are working in groups so you need to think about how to share your work with others.

Here are some ideas:
- You could save the work on floppy disks.
  This may not be possible because of the size of the images. If you are using graphics on the page, they could take up a lot of memory.
- You could use email to send your work to your friend's email address as an attachment.
  The file size may be a problem. This depends on your email system.
- If you are using a network, your teacher could set up a shared area for you all to use. If so, it is important to agree a format for saving the work between you.

Activity 3
Look at each of the ways of exchanging information: on a floppy disk, by email or on a network. Make a list of advantages and disadvantages of each method.

GOOD DESIGN

A good design for your booklet is important. People are more likely to look at it if it is well designed.

Here are some points concerning layout:
- A good eye-catching design is important for the cover.
- The layout should suit the audience.
- Is your layout designed to inform?
- Use images and pictures to liven up the pages.

Activity 2

In your group, discuss the cover for the booklet. How can you make it eye-catching?

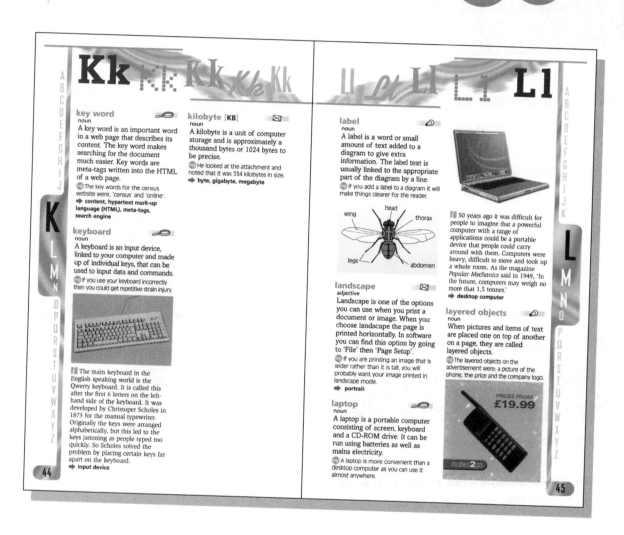

REVIEW

4 Look at the front cover of this book. How has this been made eye-catching? As a class, spend 5 minutes sharing your ideas on how to make the front cover of your booklet eye-catching.

5 A friend suggests that one easy way to share files is to have each other's passwords so that you can use each other's areas on the network. Do you think this is a good idea? Write a short passage explaining your answer.

SHOPPING IN MY TOWN

AIMS
- To think about places where visitors could shop in your town
- **To use tables to display information**
- To use a spell checker to check text

STARTER

Complete Worksheet 21.

○○ *Setting the scene*

Work on your booklet continues, and your group will now
be working as a team, adding information on places to

SHOPPING DIRECTORY

You are going to add a shopping directory to your booklet. This will provide clearly laid out information about shops and other businesses in your town. If you live in a large city, you may have too much information and will need to choose what to leave out. You should try to cover a range of shops, and say where they are and what they sell.

Activity 1

In groups, make a list of the shops you would like to include in your directory. Decide which of you will find out the information you need.

MAKING IT EASY TO READ

There are several ways you could display this information. You need a format that is easy to follow and does not contain too much information – but not too little either!
One way to do this is to use a table.

Name of shop	Type	Address	Telephone

Activity 2

This table gives some ideas about what you need to know about the shops, but what other information should be included?

There are lots of features you can change in a table:
- The style of the lines
- The width of the columns
- The alignment of text in the cells
- The depth of the rows

SPELLING

You now need to think about the presentation of your booklet and the final touches. Some DTP packages do not have spell checkers. That's because the text should be prepared before in a word processor and then imported into the DTP package.

- A **spell checker** can highlight the mistakes as you type.
- It can check the whole document when you have finished.

Spell checkers only do part of the job – they highlight words they do not recognise.

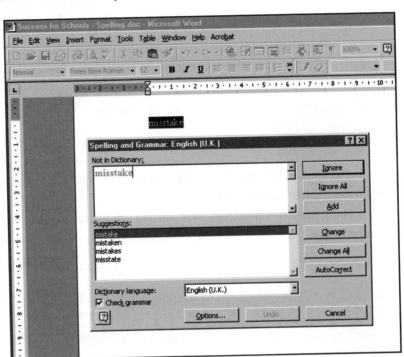

Activity 3

Load your text documents and spell check them.

The first word in the list is not always the ome you want.

Take care! It is easy to pick the wrong word.

omen
one
come
home
some

Ignore All
Add

AutoCorrect ▸
Language ▸
Spelling...

Often, spell checkers will suggest a list of words to replace your word. You will need to be careful – think about the word you need before you click the button. The first word in the list is not always the one you want.

Look at this example.

The word 'one' has been typed incorrectly. But the first word suggested by the spell checker is not the correct word.

REVIEW

4 If you key the following sentence in to a word processor, it will pass a spell check.
I no this is rite. The spell cheque tolled me sow.
As a class, spend 5 minutes discussing the problems that this shows.

5 Next, you will be adding some information about the history of your town.
To prepare for this, find out about some of the events in your town's history.
Write down a few ideas about what historical events are worth including in your
short booklet.

THE TOWN'S HISTORY

AIMS
- To add some information about the history of the town
- To use the graphic tools to draw a time line
- To examine some other DTP tools

STARTER

On your own, spend 5 minutes listing ways you can feed information into a computer.

Then, as a class, spend 5 minutes comparing your lists and producing one complete list. Were there any ways which you had not heard of before?

⊙⊙ Setting the scene

In this lesson, you will add your information about the history of your town. Next lesson, you will produce the booklet.

HISTORY OF YOUR TOWN

To make it more interesting for visitors, one page of your booklet is to be about the history of your town.

Think about what you could include:
- A photograph of one of the oldest buildings
- An old map scanned in
- Something about well-known people associated with your town

Activity 1

In small groups, look at the material you have collected already and decide which items to use in your booklet.

DISPLAYING INFORMATION

How are you going to display the information?
- In a table?
- As ordinary written text?

| How about a time line? | A **time line** will show a brief history in a way that is easy to follow. You can make it look good with some pictures. Here is an example of the kind of thing you could do. |

1320

Evidence of early settlement

REVIEW

4 As a class, spend 5 minutes looking at some of the problems you had making your time line. Describe how you overcame them.

5 Write a few sentences describing these terms: headings, subheadings, columns, boxes, body text.

WORKING WITH DIFFERENT SOFTWARE

During this project, you may have done some of the work at home, and saved it on floppy disk.

Sometimes, when you use different packages to save your work, you will have problems. You save a perfect piece of work at home but, at school, it looks like this.

Why is this? The two packages are not saving the information in the same way.

Fortunately, there are at least two ways around this:

● When you save your work, choose the option to save as <u>RTF (rich text format)</u>.
● Another way is to use text only.

It is better to use RTF. This will keep all the fonts and underlining you have used. Text only files cannot do this. All they keep are the words.

TOOLS FOR THE TIME LINE

To make a time line, you will need to use some of the drawing tools either from your drawing package or your DTP software:

● *A line drawing tool* ● *Imported graphics*
● *A crop tool* ● *Text boxes*

Most of these will be on a tool bar on your software. It might look something like this:

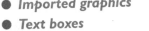

Line tool   **Text box**

Crop tool

Activity 3

Find out how to do these things using your DTP package:
☐ Turning on the drawing tools
☐ Cropping and resizing an image
☐ Drawing a line
☐ Drawing a text box

1530

St Peter's church built

1720

Battle fought nearby

1870

Visit by Queen Victoria

Activity 2

Using the information you have about your town, design a simple time line for your booklet.

Follow the mouse
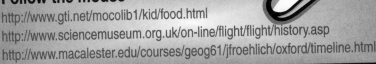
http://www.gti.net/mocolib1/kid/food.html
http://www.sciencemuseum.org.uk/on-line/flight/flight/history.asp
http://www.macalester.edu/courses/geog61/jfroehlich/oxford/timeline.html

PUTTING IT ALL TOGETHER

AIMS
- To put the finishing touches to the booklet
- To look at possible printing problems and to print it
- To evaluate another group's booklet

STARTER

⊙⊙ Setting the scene

In this final lesson on the booklet, you will put the finishing touches to it and print it.

The information that a computer gives out is called <u>output</u>. Spend 5 minutes listing all the types of output from a computer.

Lots of pieces of computer equipment can output the data. These are called <u>output devices</u>. As a class, spend 5 minutes making a list of as many output devices as you can.

DUPLEX PRINTING

Activity 3

Find out how to use duplex printing on your printer. Write some notes on how to do it.

The pages of your booklet will need to be printed on both sides of the paper. This is called <u>duplex printing</u>.

Some printers can do duplex printing if they have the right attachment. If not, you will have to print on one side of the paper and then put it back in to print on the other side. This sounds simple, but unfortunately it may not be!

Different printers will need the paper putting back in different ways. One way to tell how is to do a test print with a pencil mark on one corner of the paper then see which way it needs to be put back in. You will have to find out which way up to put the paper and which way round.

If your printer is on a network, make sure you are the only one printing. Otherwise, you may have someone else's work appearing within your booklet.

FINAL CHECKS

Before printing, you need to do some final checks:
- Is the information accurate?
- Is the spelling correct?
- Is the grammar correct?
- Check the page layout using **print preview**.
- Check that the pages are in the correct order.

Activity 1
It's often hard to spot your own mistakes. So, take one or two pages each that someone else in the group has produced and check them over.

PRINT LAYOUT

Your work will need to be printed in the form of a folded booklet like this.

Printing the pages so they are in the right order when folded into a booklet may not be straightforward. If you tell your DTP software that you want a booklet, it should be able to help with the layout of the pages. Some printers are also able to work out what order to print the pages for you.

If you have both a printer and a DTP package capable of deciding the layout, it is important you only set up one of them. Otherwise, between them, they may make a mess of it! If neither of them can, then you will have to work it out yourself.

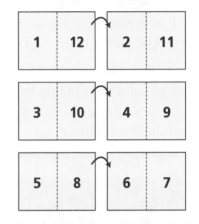

Activity 2
Find out if your DTP package or printer will do the layout, and how to set them up.

1	12	2	11
3	10	4	9
5	8	6	7

EVALUATION

It is now time to judge the completed booklet. One way is to give your booklet to someone else and to ask for their comments:
- *Does the cover catch the eye?*
- *Is the content what they are looking for?*
- *Is it interesting?*
- *Is it well laid out?*
- *Is there anything they think needs adding?*

Activity 4
Swap booklets with another group and write a list of comments about their booklet.

REVIEW

5 As a class, spend 5 minutes discussing the good points of each other's booklets and possible ideas for improvements.

6 Using the information you have from *other* members of your class, write about 100 words evaluating your *own* booklet.

COMPUTER MODELS

AIMS

- **To look at how computers can model real life, using numbers to represent real situations**
- **To look at different types of data**
- **To enter some data, use a formula and a function, and practise some spreadsheet techniques**

STARTER

⊙⊙ Setting the scene

This unit looks at how computers can model real life. In the first three lessons, you will learn about how spreadsheets can be used for modelling.

Spend about 5 minutes on this activity.
Load your spreadsheet software:

- Notice that it is laid out like a table or a grid.
- It is made up of **rows** and **columns**.
- It also has a **toolbar** and a **menu**.
- When you hold the mouse **cursor** over a button on the toolbar, a **tool tip** tells you what it is for.

Look at the toolbar buttons in your spreadsheet software. Now load your presentation software and make a note of any toolbar buttons that are the same in both packages.
As a class, spend about another 5 minutes discussing why some toolbar buttons are the same and some are different.

GETTING STARTED

Each 'box' in a spreadsheet is called a **cell**. Each cell has an **address**. You can tell what the address is by looking at the letter at the top of the column and the number at the left. So, the top left cell is cell A1. What is the address of the cell pointed to in Figure 1?

You can click in a cell and type something. You can move on to another cell using the mouse, or more quickly by using the arrow keys.

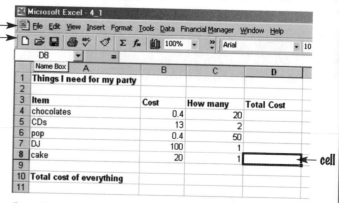

Figure 1

Activity 1

Type in the information shown in Figure 1 into a spreadsheet. Make sure everything goes in exactly the right cells and that you copy it *exactly*.

- Select Row 1 by clicking the grey box labelled **1**.
- Click the **B** button to make the row bold.
- Repeat for rows 3 and 10.

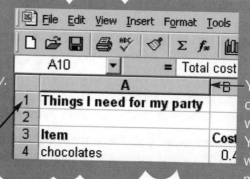

You will find that column **A** isn't wide enough. You can drag it wider with the mouse.

DATA TYPES

You have keyed in some costs of things you might need for a party. For you, this is information about the party. The computer does not know that this is about a party. To the computer, this is just __data__. The computer does know that not all data is the same, and here it has recognised two __data types__:

- *Words (text)*
- *Numbers (numeric)*

Look at how the data you keyed in has been displayed. Some is aligned to the left of its cell, some to the right. What is the difference in the data?

Activity 2

On a blank part of the spreadsheet, key this data – one item per cell:

- 17.5
- £45.99
- 012142312343
- 23/8/02

Describe how each item of data is displayed. What types of data do you think each one is? Did anything odd happen?

FORMULAE

In a spreadsheet, calculations can be done using a formula.

What happens? Click on cell D4 and write down the formula. Now click on cell D5. What is the difference between the two formulae?

Activity 3

Go to cell D4. Key in =B4*C4
Press *Enter* or an arrow key. The spreadsheet multiplies the cost by the number and displays the answer.
Click on cell D4 again. Drag the bottom right corner of the box down to cell D8.

File Edit View Insert Format Tools Data Financial Manager Window Help

100% Arial 10

D4 = =B4*C4

	A	B	C	D	E
1	Things I need for my party				
2					
3	Item	Cost	How many	Total Cost	
4	chocolates	0.4	20	8	
5	CDs	13	2		
6	pop	0.4	50		
7	DJ	100	1		
8	cake	20	1		

drag from here

down to here

ADDING IT ALL UP

The spreadsheet can be used to add up all the individual costs. This uses a function, one called SUM.

Activity 4

Click in cell D10. Type =SUM(D4:D8)
Make sure that you do not key any spaces.
Press *Enter*.

- What happens?
- How does the function know which numbers to add up?
- All functions have brackets. What are they for?

REVIEW

5 In small groups, list other things you could use a spreadsheet for. Don't spend more than 5 minutes on this!

6 A friend of yours has sent you an email asking what a spreadsheet is. Write your reply in no more than 100 words.

FORMATTING

AIMS
- **To learn how to format data in a spreadsheet**
- To change the appearance of the data
- **To align the data in the cells**

STARTER

∞ Setting the scene

This lesson builds on your spreadsheet skills, especially the way you can decide how to present data.

When you are word processing, you can change the appearance of your text by <u>formatting</u> it. For example, you can make words **bold**.

In small groups, spend 5 minutes listing some more examples of formatting.

Spend another 5 minutes looking at the spreadsheets you set up in the last lesson. How could they be made to look better?

ROW HEIGHT

You can alter the row height by dragging the row selectors. If you want several rows to be exactly the same, it can be difficult to do this accurately by dragging.

Activity 3

Select all the rows with items in them – rows 4 to 8 – by dragging through the row selectors. Go to **Format – Row – Height** and type in 25.

FONTS AND COLOURS

In big spreadsheets, it can be difficult to spot important data, like totals.

You have already done some formatting. You widened a column and made the headings **bold**.

You can also make parts stand out by the careful use of colour. You can make a cell stand out by clicking on the <u>**fill colour**</u> button. A <u>**drop down box**</u> next to it gives you a choice of colours.

Activity 1

Load the spreadsheet you set up in the last lesson. Select the headings again by clicking the row selector. Change the font with the font selector and make the text bigger.

Find the <u>font colour</u> button and change the colour of the words.

Font Color (Light Green)

Now select the row that has the grand total in it. Change its colour.

Remember that you can find the purpose of a button by holding the mouse cursor over it.

HEADING ORIENTATION

*Headings can make the columns rather wide and this can sometimes make a sheet difficult to fit on the paper. One way is to change the **orientation**. (What does orientation mean?)*

Activity 4

Select row 3. On the menu, choose **Format – Cells – Alignment**. Enter 90 degrees for orientation. Use the autofit option to tidy the sheet again.

ALIGNMENT

The numbers in cells B4 to D8 are **aligned right**. (Look back to page 37 to see different kinds of text alignment.)
The headings above these figures are **aligned left**. It may look better to align the headings with the numbers.

Activity 5

Select cells B3 to D3. Click the right-align button.

COLUMN WIDTH

The cells don't all need to be the same size. You may want to have the widths different according to how much data is in them. You can drag the widths by using the column selectors, but there are shortcuts.

Activity 2

Select the whole sheet. The quickest way is to click on the small square at the top left of the sheet.

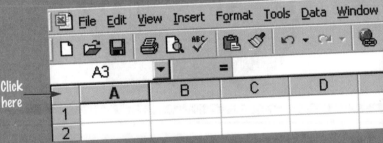

Click here

Go to the **Format** option on the menu. Select **Column** and **Autofit Selection**. What happens?

REVIEW

6 Look at Spreadsheet 1. List improvements that would make it easier to understand. Now look at Spreadsheet 2, and discuss how simple format changes can improve readability.

7 Before the next lesson, look at 2 or 3 packaged food products. Copy down the amounts of protein, carbohydrate, fat, fibre and sodium from the information given on the label.

GRAPHS AND CHARTS

AIMS

- To look at why graphs and charts are used to display data
- To see how different types of graphs suit different purposes
- To practise making charts of different types

STARTER

◯◯ Setting the scene

This lesson continues to develop your spreadsheet techniques by displaying data in graphs.

Spend about 5 minutes thinking of 3 examples of data that could be displayed as a pie chart.

Follow the mouse
http://www.usda.gov/nass/nasskids/pambio.htm
http://www.apu.edu/imt/training/excel/when_do_I_use_a_pie_chart.php

USING GRAPHS AND CHARTS

Spreadsheets can contain lots of numbers. It can be difficult to see immediately what is going on — we can miss the 'big picture'.

Graphs can be helpful to show <u>summaries</u> and <u>trends</u>.

Activity 1
WS 22
Complete Worksheet 22.

USING THE RIGHT DISPLAY

You need to select the right sort of display to show your data.

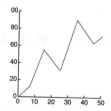

- <u>**Line graphs**</u> show trends.

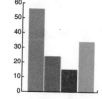

- <u>**Bar charts**</u> (column charts) can be useful when you are counting things.

Activity 2
WS 23
Complete Worksheet 23.

- <u>**Pie charts**</u> are used to show <u>proportions</u>.

MAKING A PIE CHART

Look at the food information that you collected for your last homework. Notice that the food is made from a number of different food types. A pie chart can be used to show the proportions of each food type.

- Create a chart by selecting Insert – Chart. This starts the Chart Wizard.
- Just follow the instructions to produce a pie chart.
- Add a title when asked and make the chart an object in the spreadsheet.
- Move the chart around so that it can be seen in the same screen as the data.
- Select Print – Preview to make sure that it all fits on one sheet.
  - You can re-size the pie chart if necessary.
  - Finally, print it when it is OK.

Activity 3

Load your spreadsheet software. Create a spreadsheet like the one below, using data from one of your food labels.
Select the foods and the figures to create a simple pie chart. (In the example, these are in cells A2 to B6.)

	A	B
1	Food	Amount (%)
2	Carbohydrate	56
3	Fat	24
4	Fibre	15
5	Protein	5
6	Sodium	0.1

Give your pie chart a suitable title and print it out.

MAKING A BAR CHART

Sometimes you need a chart to show the numbers of different things. A bar or column chart will show the trends well.

Activity 4

Use Worksheet 24 to practise making a bar chart.

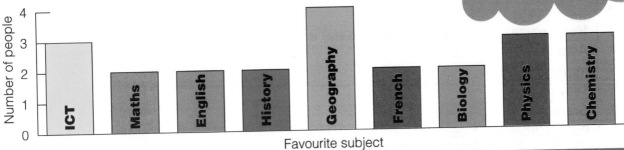

REVIEW

5 Individually, look at the Chart Wizard and list all the different types of chart and graph that are available. As a class, discuss situations where some of the graph types might be useful.

6 Decide what type of chart would be suitable to display each of these sets of data:
- The percentage of people who regularly view each television channel
- The percentage of people who vote for each party in a general election
- The number of videos hired by a shop each month
- The number of people of each eye colour

Comment on why you have chosen the type of chart in each case.

COLLECTING THE DATA 1

AIMS

- To decide what data is needed to plan a holiday
- **To see how a spreadsheet can be used to enter and sort information**
- To see how spreadsheet software can help in decision making
- To look at some websites to find some costs of a holiday

STARTER

⊙⊙ Setting the scene

This is the first of six lessons which use a spreadsheet to plan a holiday. In this lesson, you will plan what data is needed.

Spend about 5 minutes on this activity.

Imagine that you are helping your parents to plan a family holiday. Make a list of the information that you may need to help you to work out costs.

HOTEL COSTS

You might want to compare the costs of different hotels in one particular area. Here are some basic details about 5 hotels. All prices are given in pounds.

	A	B	C
1	Hotel costs		
2			
3	Hotel name	Cost per night (room) in pounds	Star rating
4	Astoria	90	4
5	Imperial	100	4
6	Seaview	85	3
7	Grand	75	2
8	Royal National	96	3

If this data is in a spreadsheet, the software can be used to check which is the cheapest hotel. It would be easy for us to do this by looking, but imagine if you had hundreds of prices to look at.

Activity 1

Enter the details about the 5 hotels into a spreadsheet.
- In cell A9, type *Cheapest price*.
- In cell B9, enter the **function** =MIN(B4:B8) and press *Enter*.

Now think of a different function you could use to make the spreadsheet find the most expensive price. Make it appear in cell B10. Make sure that this maximum price is labelled properly.

SORTING DATA

Hotels have a star rating. The more stars they have, the more facilities they offer, such as swimming pools. We can <u>sort</u> the data to show those hotels with the best – and worst – rating.

There will probably be a sort button marked A → Z on your toolbar. Alternatively, try Data – Sort.

Activity 2

Using the same spreadsheet, sort the hotel information into star rating order. Make sure that you sort all the data.

DATA FROM THE INTERNET

For some up-to-date information about hotel costs, you can look on the Internet. For example, suppose you want to find out what costs are involved in staying in a hotel in Disneyland®. Choosing any one of the Disneyland® resorts, you would want to know room charges and the costs of meals.

Activity 3

Work in pairs or small groups for this activity. Load your web browser software. Go to the address of a well-known search engine such as www.yahoo.com or www.google.com.

Type *Disneyland Hotels* into the search box. Have a look at the top 5 'hits'. Briefly discuss with others which of these hits are likely to give you information on *costs*. Quickly visit the links and follow through to see if you can find any cost information. If you are not successful after following 4 or 5 links, go back and try somewhere else.

Write a brief record of what you have found and where you it came from. Are you finding useful information yet?

REVIEW

4 A spreadsheet can be used to store a list of all the pupils in a year group and the marks they achieved in a test. Discuss different ways that the data might be sorted and give reasons. Can you think of any functions that might be useful in summarising the data?

5 Look for hotel costs in Disneyland® from some other sources. List other ways of finding the information that you need. Write a brief comment on the advantages and disadvantages of using the Internet to find this information.

COLLECTING THE DATA 2

AIMS
- To collect some data and put it into the spreadsheet
- To have more practice of using formulae and functions
- To show amounts of money with a £ sign

STARTER

⊙⊙ Setting the scene

Having started to plan a holiday, you will now sort out some data to put into a spreadsheet and arrange it tidily.

Spend about 5 minutes making a list of words that have something to do with spreadsheets.

As a group, spend another 5 minutes looking at these words and see how many refer to things that you have done already.

SIFTING THROUGH INFORMATION

When we are looking for information, it can come in all kinds of different ways. It often takes some thought before we can really see what we need. We often need to process the information before we can make comparisons.

Activity 1

Look at Worksheet 25.
The information is presented in various ways.
Sift through it so that you can compare prices between the different hotels.
Produce a summary on paper or on computer.
Use ideas from the table on Worksheet 25 to help you.

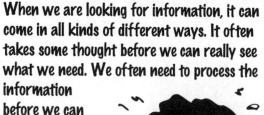

ENTERING DATA

Looking at all this information may make you feel hungry! Spreadsheet software can be useful for working out pizza prices for lunch.

Activity 2

Enter this data into a new spreadsheet.

	A	B	C	D	E
1	Name of pizza	Small	Regular	Large	Extra topping
2	Margarita	4.5	6.5	8	1
3	Hungarian	4.8	6.8	8.5	1
4	Mexican	4.85	7	8.8	1

Add one extra column and using formulae and functions, make the spreadsheet show how much it would cost to buy 4 small Margaritas, 2 large Hungarian with extra topping and 1 regular Mexican.

DISPLAYING MONEY DATA

The amounts of money entered into the spreadsheet show as numbers like 7 instead of £7.00. If you want the £ signs to show, you must not type £ signs. If you do, the spreadsheet will think you have entered text and will not be able add up the amounts of money.

Activity 3

Still using the pizza spreadsheet, drag through with the mouse to select the cells that contain amounts of money. Then choose one of these three ways:
- ☐ Select Format – Cells – Number – Decimal places – 2.
- ☐ Select Format – Cells – Currency.
- ☐ Click the currency button on the toolbar.

You can choose different currency options. What are they?

REVIEW

4 You have used the Format – Cells option to present the sums of money correctly. This would produce different results in different countries. What other formatting operations might vary in the same way? Make a class list.

5 Look in the window of a bank or post office or find out from the Internet or television what £1 is worth in terms of dollars, euros and yen. Try to find details of any other currency exchange rates.

SETTING UP A SPREADSHEET

AIMS
- **To look at how to deal with data that changes**
- To set up a spreadsheet as a currency converter
- **To learn about absolute cell addressing**
- To learn how naming cells makes it easier to construct formulae

STARTER

⬤⬤ Setting the scene
This lesson builds on your spreadsheet skills and introduces some new techniques.

Spend about 5 minutes on this activity.
You are planning a holiday. What costs might change between when you first plan your holiday and when you finally arrive at your destination? Make a list of costs that are hard to predict. As a group, see how many surprises there might be.

CONVERTING SPENDING MONEY

A family of four is planning to go to Disneyland® in Florida. Each of them has put aside a certain amount of spending money. Mum has put aside £500, Dad £200, Karl £150 and Susan £160.

	A	B	C
1	Person	Pounds	Dollars
2	Mum	500	
3	Dad	200	
4	Karl	150	
5	Susan	160	

They want to know how many dollars this is worth now. When they go on holiday, it might be worth a different amount, because the <u>exchange rate</u> often changes.
Let's assume for now that £1 (pounds sterling) is worth US$1.55787 (US dollars).
A spreadsheet can be used to convert the sterling amounts to other currencies.

Activity 1
Set up a spreadsheet showing the four people's names, and the amount of spending money (in pounds) that they have each set aside.
Make your headings bold and right align the pounds and dollars headings.
Go to a cell away from the main data, let's say cell A10.
Type in 'Rate'. Next to it, in cell B10, type 1.55787.
Now, next to Mum's money, in cell C2, type the formula =B2*B10
Press *Enter*. What happens?

Follow the mouse
http://www.xe.net/ucc/

COPYING CELLS USING FILL DOWN

The <u>fill down</u> facility copies a formula to other cells. One way to do this is to click on the cell you want to copy, then drag the bottom right corner down to the last cell you want.

Normally, when a formula is copied, it automatically adjusts itself for the next row.

In Activity 1, having the dollar signs in the formula in cell C2 prevents the formula from adjusting. The dollar symbol before the 'B' fixes row B and the dollar symbol before '10' fixes row 10. So it always takes the conversion rate from the same cell, B10. This is called <u>absolute cell addressing</u>.

Activity 2

Use fill down to copy the cell C2 to cells C3, C4 and C5 for the other people in your spreadsheet.
Format these cells as currency and select the dollar ($) symbol for US money.

Activity 3

Use fill down again, but this time experiment by using a formula without the dollar signs, e.g.
=B2*B10
What happens?

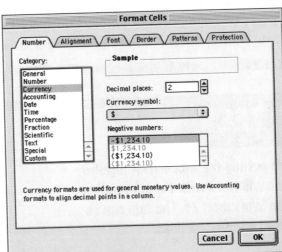

NAMING CELLS

There is a simple way to make sure that you always have information from the correct place. Instead of having to remember that the data you want is in cell B10, you could name the cell and use the name in your formula.

Activity 4

Use the same spreadsheet as in Activity 1.
Go to cell B10. From the menu, choose Insert – Name – Define. The spreadsheet will suggest the name 'Rate' because this word is next to cell B10. This is OK so accept it.
Now change the formula in C2. Type in
=B2*Rate
Fill this down and you will get the same results as before.

REVIEW

5 Look at Spreadsheet 3. Your teacher will tell you where to find it.
Work out which cells contain formulae and write down what the formulae could be.
Compare your answers with each other.

6 If you are planning to go to Disneyland®, you will have a choice of flights to go on. Find out which is your nearest airport and which airlines offer flights to
(a) Florida, (b) California and (c) Paris.

PUTTING IT TOGETHER

AIMS
- To build a spreadsheet from various pieces of information
- To practise using formulae and functions
- To practise naming cells

STARTER

⊙⊙ Setting the scene

In this lesson, you use your spreadsheet skills to build a spreadsheet to show costs for a holiday.

Spend about 5 minutes on this activity.

Spreadsheets can be very large. It is useful to set aside areas for each job that needs to be done. On a piece of paper, set out where you would put information about hotels, flights and spending money when you are planning a holiday.

HOTELS

To start putting the information together, first you will work with the information given on Worksheet 25. The data can be subdivided into four sections:
- Hotels
- Flights
- Meals
- Spending money

Later, you can later adapt the spreadsheet to use your own data if you want.

WS 25

	A	B	C
1	Holiday Planner		
2			
3	Nights	7	
4	Rooms	2	
5	Number of people	4	
6			
7	**Name of hotel**	**Single**	**Cost**
8	Hotel Astoria	80	
9	Marine Hotel	50	
10	Strathmore Hotel	70	
11			
12	Cheapest		

Activity 1

Load your spreadsheet software.
Start a new spreadsheet file.
Save it under the name 'holiday'.

In cell A1, type 'Holiday Planner'.
Make the heading stand out by using colours and suitable fonts.
- In cell B3, key in the number of nights.
- In cell B4, key in the number of rooms.
- In cell B5, key in the number of people coming on holiday.

Name these cells *Nights* and *Rooms* and *Number_of_People* so you can refer to them by name in your formulae.
Put a formula in cell C8 to work out the cost of rooms for the number of people we have and for the right number of nights.
=B8*Rooms*Nights
Copy this formula down for the other hotels.
Put a function in C12 to find the cheapest hotel.

Use the MIN function. **> go**

FLIGHTS

For information about flights, the number of people is important.

	A	B	C
15	**Flights**	**Return per person**	**Total cost**
16	British Airways	375	1500
17	Virgin Atlantic	348	1392
18	United Airlines	425	1700
19			
20	**Cheapest**		1392

Activity 2

Enter the extra data for flights in cells A15 to C20, including the functions to calculate the total cost and to show the cheapest option.

SPENDING MONEY

The same spreadsheet can be used to record the amounts of spending money that members of the family decided to take.

	A	B
23	**Spending money**	
24	**Person**	**Pounds**
25	Mum	500
26	Dad	200
27	Karl	150
28	Susan	160
29		
30	Total spend	

Formulae can then be used to work out the total amount of money that the family will need.

Activity 3

Enter the details of spending money in cells A23 to B30. Use a combination of a function (to add up the spending money) and a formula (to add in the cheapest flight and hotel prices) to calculate the final result.
Make sure all the cells that contain money are in currency format.
Then, save the spreadsheet.
Use the filename 'holiday' again.

REVIEW

4 Write 1 sentence to define each of these terms: formula, cell, function, sorting. Your teacher will ask some of you to read your sentences. As a class, agree on a final definition of each word.

5 List some ways in which you think a spreadsheet could be used for planning costs.

TESTING

AIMS

- To recognise the importance of checking that data from a computer is meaningful
- **To see how the software can sometimes help you to discover errors**
- To recognise when the software will not notice errors
- To learn what is meant by a logic error

STARTER

Work out these in your head.
Do not use a calculator or a computer.

⊙ *Setting the scene*
Your spreadsheet is now complete so, in this lesson, you do some tests to make sure that it gives you correct answers.

£21 divided by 3

If 1 euro is worth 60p, how many euros do you get for £6?

£31.50 less than £100

£41.50 plus 70p

The cost of two double rooms at £81.50 each per night for two nights

AUTOMATIC FORMULA CHECKS

It is easy to make a mistake when setting up a spreadsheet.
Some mistakes are not allowed and the spreadsheet warns you. These are called **automatic formula checks**. This makes some of your checking easy.

- You cannot put in a formula that refers to itself: a **circular reference**.
- You cannot put in a formula that tries to add words instead of numbers.

Neither of these are allowed, because they do not make sense.

Activity 1

Start a new spreadsheet.
Enter the number 4 in cell A1 and the number 5 in cell A2.
Now, in cell A3, enter the formula =A1+A2+A3.
Press *Enter*. What error message do you see?
Now, change cell A3 to 'Felicity'.
In cell A4, type =A1+A2+A3.
What error message do you see this time?

LOGIC ERRORS

Sometimes mistakes are made that are not spotted by the automatic formula checks. If an answer looks wrong but there is no warning message, the error is most likely a <u>logic error</u>.

For example, there may be a mistake in a formula – the computer may be adding up the wrong figures. This kind of mistake is quite hard to find.

Activity 2

Suppose three people have dinner and they decide to share the cost equally. They want to add together all three costs and divide by 3.

First, make sure that your spreadsheet is empty.
One way to do this is to select all the cells with data in and press the **Delete** key (not the **Backspace**).
In cells A1 to A3, enter 5.45, 6.3 and 7.32.
In cell A4, enter the formula =A1+A2+A3/3.
Does the answer make sense? Is it right to ask each person to pay £14.19?
Notice that the spreadsheet first divided 7.32 by 3, *then* added the sums together.
If there is a multiply or a divide to do, that will be done *before* any additions or subtractions. Using brackets solves this problem.
The formula =(A1+A2+A3)/3
forces the additions to be done first, and that gives the correct answer.
Amend the formula and check it works.

REVIEW

3 Look at Spreadsheet 4.
Identify all the errors. Describe ways that these errors could have been avoided. Now look at Spreadsheet 5.

4 Make sure you have a printed copy of your holiday costs spreadsheet. List tests you could carry out to make sure that it is set up correctly.

FINISHING TOUCHES

AIMS

- To see how a spreadsheet can be used to check what will happen in different circumstances – 'what if?' exercises
- To use a spreadsheet to make a decision: whether a family can afford a holiday
- To make some summary charts and paste them into a report

STARTER

The Disneyland® holiday will cost a lot of money. In small groups, spend a few minutes thinking of ways in which it could be made cheaper. Also, think of a few ways you could spend an extra £1000 on the holiday.

∞ Setting the scene

This final lesson looks at whether you can afford a holiday. You will use the spreadsheet model to ask 'what if?' questions and present your findings in a report.

WHAT IF?

What if there were some more money? What could the family do? What if the family had to cut back? Could they still go on holiday? The spreadsheet can provide the answers to these questions very quickly.

Activity 1

Load your spreadsheet software and the 'holiday' spreadsheet file. You should have some space below row 30.

- ☐ In cell A32, type *Budget*. That is how much we think we can afford.
- ☐ In cell B32, type 3000.
- ☐ In cell A33, type *Balance*. This is how much we will have left over if we spend less than the budget.
- ☐ In cell B33, type the formula =B32-B30

You should see a negative result – too much has been spent!

You can now make changes on the spreadsheet to try and 'balance the books'.

- ☐ *What if* mum only takes £300 spending money? Make the change and see what happens to the balance.
- ☐ Mum might not like that, so what else could she do?
- ☐ Make some changes based on the ideas you came up with in the starter activity.
- ☐ *What if* Uncle Lou gives you all an extra £1000? Could you afford a better hotel? Try it out.

PRESENTING YOUR FINDINGS

You can now produce a professional-looking report showing your recommendations about the holiday and why you made them.

Follow the mouse
http://www.functionx.com/access/lesson15.htm

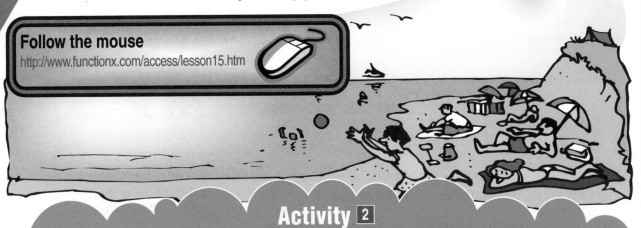

Activity 2

Have your word processor and spreadsheet software loaded. In the word processor, type the headline *The Holiday Report*. Choose a large font and use colour to make it stand out. Write a couple of paragraphs explaining what your aims were and where you found the information on holiday costs.

Switch to your spreadsheet. Make a bar chart to show how the total costs of the hotels compared. You can do this by selecting cells A8 to A10, then hold down the control key and highlight cells C8 to C10. Select the chart wizard and produce the chart as an embedded object in the sheet. Make sure you label the chart and the chart axes.

Change the size of the chart so that you can easily read it. You may have to change the size of the font (double click on the y-axis and you will see a suitable **dialogue box** to help you). Make sure that the drawing tools are available (View – Toolbars – Drawing). Then use a text box and an arrow to point out the cheapest hotel.

Select the whole chart by clicking near its edge and copy it (use the menu or Ctrl-c). Go back to your report and position the cursor where you want the chart. Paste it in (menu or Ctrl-v). It should look something like this:

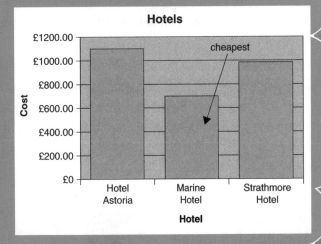

Do the same with the flights information and finally round off with a summary of what you propose. Make sure that the whole report looks good and has no spelling mistakes.

REVIEW

3 As a class, list situations where you could use a spreadsheet to do a '*what if?*' investigation. What data would you need?

4 Suppose you were given £1000 to furnish and decorate a bedroom. What would you spend it on? Would you be able to do all that you wanted? Try to find some realistic figures. You may want to try it on a spreadsheet later.

DATABASES

AIMS
- To look at the importance of market research
- To find out what a database is and also what a database management system does

STARTER

WS 26

Look at the advert for a new mobile phone on Worksheet 26. As a class, spend 5 minutes discussing the advert.

- Who do you think it is aimed at? Explain your answer.
- How does the company find out what people want?

Setting the scene

This first lesson on databases introduces a new topic: the design of a mobile phone.

MARKET RESEARCH

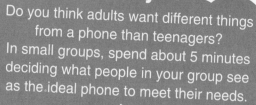

When a company is about to launch a new product, it spends a lot of time and money doing market research.

Market research helps the company to decide who will buy the product, at what price, and what their expectations of the product are. The company may want to collect information from one particular type of person, e.g. teenagers. Or it may want information from a range of people.

All the information needs to be carefully stored and analysed.

Follow the mouse
http://phones4u.co.uk/

Activity 2
Do you think adults want different things from a phone than teenagers?
In small groups, spend about 5 minutes deciding what people in your group see as the ideal phone to meet their needs.

DATABASES AND DATABASE SOFTWARE

A _database_ is a carefully organised store of data on a computer system.

Database software is designed to store data in a way that makes it easy to sort and search. Database software is able to handle very large amounts of data very quickly. It can also display information in many different ways.

It is important that the data you put into a database is accurate. Otherwise, your results will be wrong.

Activity 4
What do you think are the advantages of using a database compared with storing data on paper?
Can you think of any disadvantages?
Write down 3 advantages and 3 disadvantages.

MOBILE PHONE DESIGN

A mobile phone company is thinking about introducing a new mobile phone range. It would like your class to carry out some research and to present some information to help them with the design of the range.

Activity 1

What information do you think the mobile phone company needs?
Make of list of some of the things they need to find out.

COLLECTING AND STORING INFORMATION

To do this topic well, you will need to collect and store a lot of data. It may be a good idea to work with others in your class and to pool all your data. Before you collect any data, you need to think about what you are going to do with it.

Computers can be very useful for handling large amounts of data. They can be used to sort, search, count and display data in many different ways.

The software you are going to use is called a **database management system**.

Activity 3

Find out what database management software is available on your school system. Is it available on all the computers or just some of them? Who is allowed to use it?

REVIEW

5 As a class, spend a few minutes discussing how a database might be helpful in your mobile phone project.

6 Before this book was published, a lot of market research was done. If you were to do market research for a book like this, who would you contact, and what questions would you ask?

QUESTIONNAIRES

AIMS

- To look at collecting data
- To look at how forms should be designed
- To write good questions

STARTER

On your own, spend about 5 minutes looking at the questions on Worksheet 27.

- Are they easy to follow?
- Could you answer them?
- Could you make the questions better?

Then, as a class, spend another 5 minutes discussing how you could improve the questions.

∞ Setting the scene

In this lesson, you will decide how to collect data about mobile phone features, to be put into a database.

METHODS OF COLLECTING DATA

Before you can put any information into a computer, you need to collect it.

Activity 1

Make a list, suggesting other ideas for collecting information for research.

Think about how the phone company might collect data for its market research. There are plenty of choices.

- Send out questionnaires.
- Do a survey by telephoning people to ask questions.
- Interview people.
- Look at what other companies are doing.
- Analyse the sales of existing products.

DESIGN THE FORM

If you are using a questionnaire, you need to look carefully at how it is designed. It must be clear and quick to fill in.

- *Use boxes like this.*

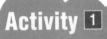
Surname ☐☐☐☐☐☐☐☐☐

- *Use tick lists to make it quick.*

Have you a mobile at the moment?   Yes ☐   No ☐

- *Use a clear font to make it easy to read.*

Activity 4

You are producing a form to send to lots of people. Produce a design on paper for your form to collect the following information:
- ☐ Do they have a mobile phone already?
- ☐ What make do they have?
- ☐ How long have they had a mobile phone?
- ☐ Which age group are they in?

ASKING THE RIGHT QUESTIONS

It is important to collect the information in a way that makes it easy to enter it into the database. It will slow you down if you have to think about what things mean when you are keying the data in.

It is important to ask the right questions. The person should have no doubts about what you want to know.

What do you think of red phones?

How many different ways can this question be answered?

It might be better to ask a more direct question.

Do you think red is a good colour for phones?

This can be answered 'Yes' or 'No'. It is a better question because there is little doubt about how to answer it.

However, the best question might be:

What is the best colour for a mobile? (Tick one only.)
Red ■   Yellow ■   Blue ■   Green ■

For a database to be useful to you, the questions need to have short simple answers. Questions with one-word answers, or a range of answers to choose from are the best type.

Activity 2

Write 5 simple questions you could ask about mobile phones.
Try to make up questions that only need one-word answers.

WHO IS ANSWERING THE QUESTIONS?

- Questionnaires should be as quick as possible to answer. If there are too many questions, people will give up. But make sure you still collect all the information you need.

- Think about the kind of questions being asked and how people will react to them. Some people might not like being asked their age. You can collect this kind of information by asking them to choose an age range. People often feel more comfortable with this method and it will often give you enough information.

- Try not to ask pointless questions. For example, for the mobile phone survey, do you need their name and address? What use would that be to you?

Which age range are you in?

Please tick one.

11–14	
15–19	
20–25	
25–30	
30 +	

Follow the mouse
http://www.raosoft.com/design/designtip.html

Activity 3

Make up some rules for good questions.
For example: Keep them short.

REVIEW

5 Complete Worksheet 28. As a class, discuss the good and bad points on the questionnaire.

6 List the information you need to collect to help with the design of the new phone. You will need to think about the features a phone might have.

INTERVIEWS

AIMS
- To look at interviews and forms
- To learn about keeping data safe

STARTER

Someone at the phone company has suggested that teenagers are only interested in how many logos they can have on their phones and how many ring tones they can have.

What kind of information would you need to collect to see if this is a correct statement?

As a class, discuss the type of questions that you need to help you.

⊙⊙ Setting the scene
You have written questions for a questionnaire on mobile phone features. Now the use of interviews is considered as a way of collecting data.

USING INTERVIEWS

Another way to collect information is to interview people. You can then fill in a form as they answer the questions.

Activity 2
Think of 2 more advantages and disadvantages of interviews.

ADVANTAGES	DISADVANTAGES
Fewer errors will be made filling in the form.	It takes up more of your time.
You will make sure the form is complete.	You need to be careful not to influence the answers.

KEEPING DATA SAFE

To a large company, the data from market research is valuable:

- It costs money to collect.
- It can be used to develop a new product which might make the company a lot of money.

What if something goes wrong? Computers sometimes break down and then the data can be lost.

How can you help?

- If the data is important, keep more than one copy.
- If you use passwords, keep them to yourself.

Activity 4
Write a set of rules for keeping data safe.

USING FORMS

Activity 1

Think of 2 more advantages and disadvantages of forms.

A well-designed form can make collecting information very easy.

ADVANTAGES	DISADVANTAGES
You can send them to lots of people.	Not all the forms you send out will come back.
People can fill them in, in their own time.	People could fill them in wrongly.
You can enter the data into the database very easily.	You may not be able to read some of them.

TIPS

- Include a heading on the form
- Ask for capital letters to be used
- Use tick boxes where suitable ☑
- Use spaces for letters e.g. Postcode ☐☐☐☐☐☐☐
- Include instructions for returning the form

STORING DATA AND THE LAW

Activity 3

Find out 2 things a company must do if the Data Protection Act applies to its data.

If a company is going to store personal data on a computer, it must comply with the Data Protection Act. This sets out rules about what can and cannot be done with the data.

The Data Protection Act only applies if you can identify someone from the data. So, in market research, if you do not have any names and addresses in the data and you cannot identify anyone, the Data Protection Act does not apply.

Follow the mouse:
http://www.dataprotection.gov.uk/principl.htm

REVIEW

5 As a class, spend 5 minutes looking at how data might be damaged or lost. List as many examples as you can.

6 The phone company wants to display a poster to its staff about keeping data safe. Design a poster for them.

WHAT INFORMATION?

AIMS

- **To look at outputs – what do we want to find out?**
- To consider the reasons for collecting data
- To design a questionnaire
- To look at the aims of research

STARTER

As a class, make a list of features you might look for in a mobile phone.

Using this information, discuss how this might be of use to the company in designing a new phone.

⚭ Setting the scene

Having looked at using forms and interviews to collect data, this lesson concentrates on what you want to find out.

DISPLAYING RESULTS

Activity 2

- Give some examples of numerical information.
- Give some examples of information that will fit into groups.

You have to bear in mind the way you intend to display your results. This can affect how you need to collect the data.

Not all information is good for making graphs and charts. If you need graphs, it is best to collect numerical information.

This means you need to have the kind of information that can be grouped, or counted in some way. If you have too many different answers to a question, a graph can be meaningless.

Makes of mobile phones

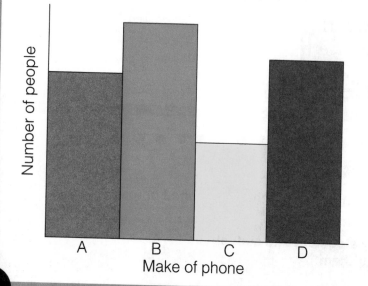

Mobile phone usage

THE RESEARCH

Remember that the reason for this research is to find out what people would like in a mobile phone. We must not waste time collecting information we do not need. If we know what we are looking for, we can ask the right questions.

Activity 1

Write down 3 things you want to find out about from this research.

What the designer needs to know
- Size
- Ring tones
- Internet access
- Picture messaging
- Predictive text
- Logos
- Covers
- Hands free
- Battery life
- Car charger

THE NEXT STEPS

Activity 3

Design your questionnaire to collect the information.

Before you design your questionnaire, check these things:
- **Decide what information you need to collect.**
- **Make sure you know why you are collecting that information.**
- **Make sure you know what you will produce from that information.**

REVIEW

4 Ask another group to spend 5 minutes looking at your questionnaire. Ask them to suggest improvements to the layout and the question style.

5 As a class, spend 5 minutes listing the most common improvements suggested.

6 You should now have a questionnaire ready to be used. Take some away at the end of the lesson and fill them in, ready for the next lesson.

SETTING UP A DATABASE

AIMS
- To look at how a database is set up, and its basic structure of fields and records
- To learn about data types

STARTER

As a group, spend about 5 minutes making a list of advantages and disadvantages of using a computer system for storing data.

∞ Setting the scene
You have now collected some data, so in this lesson, you start to think about how the data can be stored, in a database.

DATA TYPES

Computers treat words and numbers differently, just like we do. However, computers cannot work out which is which. We have to tell them how to deal with each field. To do this, we use **data types**.

Activity 2
Complete Worksheet 30.
WS 30

Data type	
Text	Anything that can be typed, such as letters or letters and numbers, e.g. someone's name or a postcode.
Number	Use this for numbers, especially when you need to do calculations or put things in numerical order, e.g. the number of doors on a car.
Date	There is a special type for dates and times, e.g. 23/9/2002.
Yes/No	Has a member paid the bill? Yes or no.

SETTING UP THE FIELDS

A database has to be set up before you can use it.

You are going to set up a database for the information from your forms.

- Try to set up one field for each question.
- Decide on the data type for that field.
- Try to have only one word or number for each answer.
- You can save time and space by using codes for some of the data such as M for male and F for Female.

Activity 4
Look at your questionnaire and decide on the data type for each of your fields. You will also have to give each field a name so decide this at the same time.

WHAT IS A DATABASE?

A **database** is a collection of data on a computer system. It is organised in a way that makes finding and sorting the data easier.

This collection of cards represents the database.

Each person has a card, called a <u>record</u>. Each card has 3 pieces of information on it. These are called <u>fields</u>.

Surname: Patel

Surname: Kapoor

Surname: Jones
First name: Fred
Form: 7A

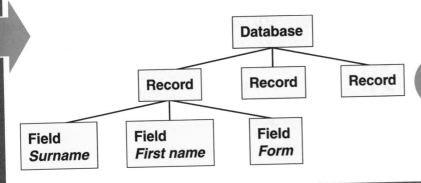

Activity 1 — WS 29
Complete Worksheet 29.

CHOOSING DATA TYPES

You need to think carefully to select the most appropriate data type.
Look at these examples.

Activity 3
Load your database software and make a list of the data types it has available.

Example	What is the data?	What data type?
23 Windows Road	This is an address, but which data type should be used when data includes both numbers and letters?	Store this data as text. Text can be a mixture of numbers and letters.
0769 688 5724	This is a telephone number, so should it be stored as a number in a computer?	Numbers do not normally start with a zero. They do not have spaces in them. If someone asks you for your telephone number you do not say 'four hundred and fifty four thousand eight hundred and ninety five'.

Telephone numbers should be stored as text. |

REVIEW

5 As a class, spend 5 minutes discussing any difficulties you had in deciding on data types.

6 Write a short passage explaining about the different data types you have used in your own database. Make sure you say why you chose each one.

ENTERING DATA

AIMS
- **To enter data into a database**
- **To learn about validation rules, accuracy and word lists**

STARTER

Use Worksheet 31 for this activity.

⚭ Setting the scene
You have collected lots of data, and set up your database. In this lesson, you will enter the data and learn some database techniques.

ACCURACY

People use databases because they produce accurate results very quickly. It is important to make sure that the data you give to a computer is accurate.

Activity 1
Complete Worksheet 32.

A database cannot give good results if the data is wrong. Remember the IT expression: *GIGO* (garbage in garbage out).

USING LISTS OF DATA

When you designed your form, you tried to give the user only a limited choice of answers.

Activity 4
Find out how to set up word lists in your database.

What is the most important use for your mobile phone? (Tick one answer.)	
Business	
Pleasure	
Safety	

When you enter this data, you will only type in one of these 3 words. To save more time and to make it very accurate, you can set up most database software to give you a list of words to choose from. One way is to use a **combo box** like the one on the right.

This makes it quicker, and reduces the chances of errors because of poor typing.

COMMON MISTAKES

It is easy to make mistakes when you key in data. Some are easier to spot than others. Here are some common mistakes and some ideas on how to avoid them.

- When typing words, it is easy to miss out letters or misspell a word. You should read the word very carefully before typing it in. Using codes like M for Male and F for female also helps with accuracy – it is difficult to misspell one letter!

- When you type in numbers, it is easy to key the digits the wrong way round. For example, you might type in 15 instead of 51. Look at the data carefully as you enter it.

Activity 2
Complete Worksheet 33.
WS 33

VALIDATION

A computer can be programmed to help you to avoid some mistakes. When it stops you from entering data that is not sensible and making silly errors, this is called <u>validation</u>.

With validation, you give the computer a set of rules to test the data as you enter it. If you break the rules, the computer will tell you.

Dates	In most databases, if you set up a field to be a date type, the computer will check if it is a sensible date. If you try to put in something like 30/02/2030, the software will warn you, because this date does not exist.
Numbers	When working with numbers, you can set up a <u>range check</u>. This means that the number must fit between a lowest and highest value. For example, when choosing lottery numbers, they must be no less than 1 and no more than 49.

Activity 3
Look at the data you have collected for your mobile phone survey. Make a list of rules you can use for some of the fields.

REVIEW

5 As a class, spend 5 minutes discussing the rules you have set for your data. Think of examples from other databases where different rules might apply.

6 How do you tell if a date makes sense? List some rules to check that a date is reasonable.

ASKING QUESTIONS

AIMS
- **To look at simple ways of searching and sorting the database**
- **To consider some examples of complex searches**

STARTER

Use Worksheet 34 for this activity.

WS 34

⊙⊙ *Setting the scene*
This lesson introduces more database techniques and considers again the importance of accuracy.

ACCURACY

Accuracy is important when entering data. It is also important when setting up queries. Ask the wrong question and the answer will be wrong too!

Remember that computers are very accurate. If you search for people called 'Anne', the list would not include those people called 'Ann' or those you entered as 'ANNE'. The database treats all these examples as different names.

You also need to think about how the question is asked.

A search for people aged 10 AND aged 50 will give no results. People cannot be *both* 10 and 50.

What you want here is people aged 10 OR 50.

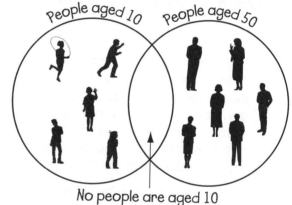

People aged 10   People aged 50

No people are aged 10 <u>and</u> aged 50

Activity 2
Complete Worksheet 35.

WS 35

COMPLEX SEARCHES

Remember how when you search for things on the Internet, the words AND and OR can be used.

Those words can also be used in complex searches on a database.

Activity 3
Complete Worksheet 36.

WS 36

| AND | This narrows a search by including both conditions in a search. For a record to be selected, the conditions on each side of the word AND must be true. |
| OR | This widens a search. A record is included if either of the conditions is true. |

DATABASE TECHNIQUES

Database software can do all sorts of useful things with your data.

Here are some common tasks that people use databases for. Your database software may use **queries** to do these jobs.

Sorting	Databases can be sorted into any order, according to the data type of the field.

For fields with numbers, there are two options:
- Ascending order, with the lowest first
- Descending order, with the highest first

ascending order

Expenses
11 Jan 03	40.26
13 Jan 03	13.50
15 Jan 03	3.00
16 Jan 03	1.50
	58.26

descending order

Test Results
98	Joan Turner
96	Brian Marks
94	Jim Brown
92	Kara Little

For fields with words, there are also two options:
- Alphabetical order, from A to Z
- Reverse alphabetical order, from Z to A

alphabetical order

Telephone list
Adams	01202 136136
Brown	07791 661662
Carter	01208 991246

Searching	Databases can be searched so that only those records that match your search are displayed.

Searches can be simple:
- Find the records where 'phone use' matches the word 'safety'.
- Find the records where the phone user is female.

Searches can be complex:
- Find all the records where 'phone use' matches the word 'safety' **AND** where the phone user is female.

This produces a single list where **both** conditions are met in the same record.

Activity 1

Open your database and try some simple sorting and searching operations.

REVIEW

4 As a class, spend 5 minutes looking at the answers to Worksheets 35 and 36.

5 Using no more than 50 words, write an email to a friend explaining the difference between a search and a sort.

DATABASE REPORTS

AIMS
- **To learn about generating reports from a database**
- **To learn about field totals**
- **To transfer a report to Word**

STARTER

As a class, look at the two charts on Worksheet 37.

- What message do you think they are trying to show?

- How well do you think these charts convey the message?

- Could they be improved?

⬤⬤ Setting the scene
Last lesson, you learnt how to set up searches and sorts. This lesson looks at producing reports from databases.

USING TOTALS

One of the useful features of reports is that you can perform calculations on numerical data.

The database software can calculate things such as totals and averages and place them at the end of the report. You could, for example, display the average age of people in a section of the report.

Activity 3
Look at your data. Are there any fields that would give some meaningful totals?
Look at this example.
What does this made up data tell you about how people use phones?

Average use

age   14

number of uses per day	Gender
20	Female
50	Female
30	Male
12	Female

Average uses 28

age   40

number of uses per day	Gender
1	Female
2	Male
3	Male

Average uses 2

WHAT IS A REPORT?

Most of the work done so far has been based around producing simple lists from the database. Most database software can produce more useful output than just simple lists.

Table 2 — Title

Type of phone	Age	Number of texts per day	Gender
Nokia	14	5	Female
Nokia	15	20	Female
Ericsson	50	2	Male
Motorola	40	1	Female

Field headings

Data

Footer

04 November 2003   Page 1 of 1

A report is a better way to present your data in a printout. With a report, you can decide the size and appearance of everything that appears on the page. The information appears the way you want to see it. This means that the report can be made to suit your needs, whatever they are.

Reports can have headings, subheadings, graphics, charts and much more besides.

REPORT IDEAS

Remember that these reports are to help a mobile phone company to design a range of phones.

It would be a good idea to set up some reports displaying information collected from different age ranges.
Here are some suggestions:

- How often each age group uses a mobile phone
- What features each age groups sees as important
- Graphs showing the proportion of males and females interviewed

REVIEW

4 As a class, spend 5 minutes looking at and discussing the types of reports that might be useful to the company.

5 Draw an example of a report you could produce. On the drawing, label the headings, field titles and any other features you have used.

THE VISUAL PRESENTATION

AIMS
- **To generate ideas for a factual presentation**
- To look at what is needed in a visual presentation
- **To set up a brief presentation**

STARTER

As a class, spend about 5 minutes brainstorming ideas for the visual presentation.

Think about how you can make the presentation attractive and interesting.

⬤⬤ Setting the scene

This lesson concentrates on what is needed in the visual presentation and builds on work done earlier (Units 1 and 2).

A FACTUAL DISPLAY

We have seen that your presentation needs to take the facts into account.

As well as making recommendations, you must use the information you have obtained from the survey.

Activity 4

Set up the slides you planned in Activity 3. Remember to keep it simple and to the point.

My factual display

	1st Qtr	2nd Qtr	3rd Qtr	4th Qtr
East	20.4	27.4	90	20.4
West	30.6	38.6	34.6	31.6
North	45.9	46.9	45	43.9

You could display the results in tables, as charts or as sections cut from reports.

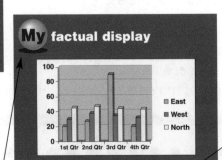

My factual display

You may decide that to have a company logo at the same position on each slide will give a consistent feel.

My factual display

Page 5 states:
North sales were steady but East's results in the third quarter were exceptional.

WHAT TO INCLUDE

The aim of this part of the project is to put together a brief factual report based on the data you collected. You should make some recommendations to the company about the design of the new phone range.

Here are some ideas about what you could include:

- Phone features, logos, text facilities
- Battery life
- Changeable cover designs

Activity 1

Make a list of other possible recommendations you could make.

USE YOUR DATA

Activity 2

Using your recommendations from Activity 1, suggest ways you could back up your argument. How could you best display the data?

To back up any ideas you have, your presentation will need to make effective use of the data you have collected.

For example, if your data suggests that younger people send a lot of text messages, then give some facts and figures to back up that statement. You could use a graph or a table to display the results.

THE AUDIENCE

This display is aimed at the directors and the design team of a large company.

They will not be impressed with fancy sounds and gimmicks.

Your display should be brief, accurate and informative.

Activity 3

Plan a display of 5 or 6 slides, setting out your ideas.

REVIEW

5 In pairs, look at the displays produced by other groups.

6 As a class, spend 5 minutes discussing how you have used your data to good effect in your presentations.

7 Write a brief evaluation of your display. Consider how well it worked and how it might have been improved.

THE FINAL REPORT

AIMS
- To look at some of the ways to produce a printed report
- To consider how the report should look

STARTER

Worksheet 38 shows a page from a report like the one you are going to produce. Spend 5 minutes looking at this and make a list of improvements that you could make.

As a class, spend about 5 minutes discussing these improvements.

⊙ Setting the scene

In this final lesson, you will produce a word-processed report of your findings.

PRINTED REPORT

The presentation that you set up was designed to put across your ideas very briefly. You now need to produce a more detailed report.
In your final report, you should present this information:

- The results of the questionnaire
- How these results led to your recommendations for the phone design.

You should display the results of the questions clearly as a graph or as a table, with the conclusion you have drawn from them clearly stated.

Activity 1
Look at your questionnaire. Make a list of the questions that provided the

You may need to use more than one question for each conclusion.

COPYING FROM A DATABASE

A lot of the information for your report can be copied from your database. With some software, you can use copy and paste. If you are using MS Office, you can transfer a report directly into Word.

Activity 4
Produce your report and your recommendations.

This is how to export your report from Access into MS Word.

- Open up your report.
- Select Tools – Office links, then click Publish It With MS Word.

The report will be transferred into a Word document. You can then work with it like any other Word document.

HEADERS AND FOOTERS

One way that you can make a document easier to follow is to add headers and footers. It is easy to do this with a word processor.

- A <u>header</u> is something added at the top of every page.
- A <u>footer</u> is something added at the bottom of every page.

In a document like this, the header could be a title such as the company name. The footer could have the date and the page numbers. It is really up to you what to put in them.

Why not put a footer or a header on *everything* you do from now on. Put your name in it and the date.

Activity 2

Load up your word processor and work out how to use the header and footers. Also find out how to put the page number on so that it changes automatically.

FORMAL DOCUMENT STYLE

This is a formal document for a large company so note these points:

- The language should be formal.
- The font should be plain, not fancy.
- Clip art and WordArt may not be suitable.

Activity 3

Suggest 3 more things that help to make a document more formal.

Tekulon plc
Pendle Industrial Park
Lowecaster
LW3 7YF
tel: 01234 567890
fax: 01234 098765

email: info@tekulon.com
website: www.tekulon.com

3 March 2003

HR Department
QAC Training
The Quad
Malsesbury Business Park
Malsesbury
ML4 2JJ

Dear Sirs

Ref IT Instructors and Consultants

We need some twenty training instructors and database consultants as soon as possible to help us implement our new stock control system. They need to be proficient in Oracle or SQL server. They should be experienced in training small numbers of professional users.

We are able to offer above market rates for their services.

If you are able to help us, I would be grateful if you could contact me as soon as possible to arrange start dates.

If you would like any further information, please do not hesitate to contact me.

Yours faithfully

Cleo T. Katt
Training Manager

REVIEW

5. As a class, spend 5 minutes discussing your findings. List the main things you need to think about when making a report.

6. Complete your report.

COMPUTER CONTROL

AIMS
- To look at how computers can control things
- To learn how to give simple instructions
- To look at how instructions are given to people
- To see how giving instructions to a computer requires far more thought

STARTER

◯◯ *Setting the scene*

This lesson introduces a new topic: how computers can control things. We start by looking at how to give simple instructions.

In small groups, make some notes about what you have to do to send a text message to a friend on your mobile phone.

When you have finished, see whether your instructions are much the same as those written down by other groups.

INSTRUCTING A COMPUTER

Computers are *much* more stupid than people. They have to be told *everything*. They also are very fussy about how they are given instructions. Make one mistake in giving instructions and the computer won't do the job you want.

Activity 2

In small groups, write down a list of different ways that you have given instructions to a computer. What did you want it to do and how did you make it happen?

Some computer software is able to make guesses about what you want if you do not express yourself very precisely, but you can never rely on that.

INSTRUCTIONS

When someone gives another person some instructions, it is possible to get away with not being very precise. We can assume that the person knows a few things already that will help to achieve a task.

For example, we can say to someone 'go and fetch that book from the table, please'. We don't normally have to say how far away the table is, what we mean by a book or how to walk over to the table.

When you do write instructions it's important that they are easy to understand.

Disconnect the tension spring from the tension unit, using manufacturer's tool P32J.

Activity 1

Try this activity in pairs. Think up a very simple task like fetching something or closing a door. Write down a series of instructions that you would give to someone who doesn't know how to do anything apart from basic movements. The other person then tries to follow the instructions but does not do anything that is not in the instructions. See how successfully the task is carried out. How difficult is it to make sure that the instructions work?

PROGRAMS

Activity 3

Have a look at some of the programs on your computer system. Write down the names of 10 of them. What is each one for? How do you know that they are programs?

Computers need instructions if they are to do the things we want them to do. We can give them instructions by writing a **computer program**. We can store the program on a disk. When we want the computer to follow the instructions, we **load** the program into **memory** and then the computer will carry out the instructions one by one.

There are lots of ways of writing computer programs. We use one of many **programming languages** to do this.

REVIEW

4 As a class, spend 5 minutes writing a set of instructions to boil a kettle of water.

5 Think of examples of instructions that are given to people in a precise step-by-step way. It may be a recipe or flat pack furniture instructions. For one example, decide whether the instructions are easy or hard to follow. Do you think the person writing the instructions makes assumptions about the person who will be carrying out the instructions?

LOGO 1

AIMS
- **To learn how a programming language can be used to give simple instructions to a computer**
- To learn some commands in the LOGO programming language
- **To use LOGO and its turtle graphics to draw simple shapes**

STARTER

There are lots of different programming languages that programmers use to give instructions to a computer. Find out if your computer or network has any. Have a look on the Internet to find the names of some programming languages.

In a group, compare your lists. Are many of your suggestions the same? Which language appeared most often?

⊙⊙ *Setting the scene*

You have already looked at giving instructions to people and computers. In this lesson, you will use a programming language to give simple instructions to a computer.

Follow the mouse:
http://howstuffworks.com

TURNING CORNERS

You make the turtle turn corners by telling it go right or left and by how many degrees.

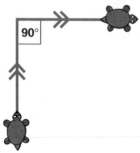

90°

Activity 2

Clear the screen. Send the turtle home and try **RIGHT 90** or **RT 90**.

- ☐ Give instructions for the turtle to draw a square.
- ☐ Now clear the screen and make the turtle draw a triangle. (Hint – an equilateral triangle is easiest).
- ☐ Make the turtle draw out the first letter of your name (don't worry about any curves for now).

LEAVING GAPS

The turtle doesn't have to leave a trail. You can switch it off with the command **PENUP (PU)**. You turn the trail on again with **PENDOWN (PD)**.

Activity 3

Give instructions to LOGO to make two squares next to each other.

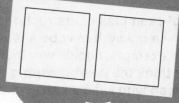

LOGO

LOGO is a very powerful programming language. You can use it to make a computer do almost anything. A good way to learn LOGO is to use it to drive a pointer around a screen, leaving a trail behind it.

The pointer is called a <u>turtle</u>. You can give it instructions by telling it to go forwards, backwards, to turn corners and many other things.

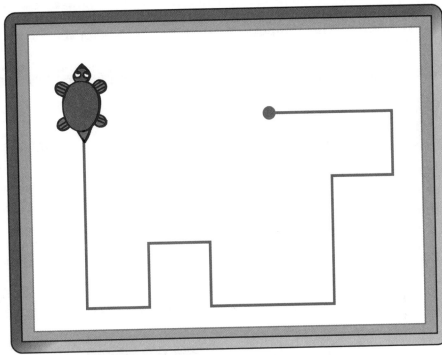

Activity 1

Load your version of LOGO.

There are lots of different versions of LOGO, so you may have to find out how your version differs from the instructions given here.

The graphics screen will display the turtle. There will be a place where you can type instructions. Send the turtle forwards a small distance. You will have to experiment to find how far to send it. Try **FORWARD 100**. 100 means one hundred turtle steps. It is important to have a space between the command **FORWARD** and the distance.

Most versions of LOGO let you abbreviate the command to **FD 100**.

Bring the turtle back with **BACKWARD 100** or **BK 100**.

If you want to start again, use the command **CLEARSCREEN** or **CS**.

If you want to bring the turtle back to the starting position, try **HOME**.

Find out how many turtle steps it is from the centre of the screen to the edge.

REVIEW

4 As a class, spend 5 minutes comparing your instructions from Activity 3. Did you all do it the same way?

5 Write a set of LOGO-like instructions to guide someone from one place to another in your home. For example, FD 10 means forward 10 steps. Test it out on someone. Draw a diagram to show the path taken and write down the instructions.

LOGO 2

AIMS

- To see how to make the instructions repeat themselves
- To see how using loops allows us to make the computer do most of the work for us
- To program the computer to work out angles for us
- To use LOGO to program loops

STARTER

When we start using a computer, we give it instructions using its operating system. Most PCs use an operating system called *Windows*. Write down how you can use *Windows* to delete any files that you don't need any more.

If you have any, now would be a good time to tidy up.

∞ Setting the scene

You have done some simple programming using LOGO. In this lesson, you will learn how to make the instructions repeat themselves.

REPEATS WITHIN REPEATS

You can enclose a repeat inside another repeat. Here's one – be careful to get it all exactly right. If you make a mistake there should be a way of making a slight change and trying again.

REPEAT 2 [REPEAT 100 [FD 50 BK 50 RT 360/100] RT 90 PU FD 200 LT 90 PD]

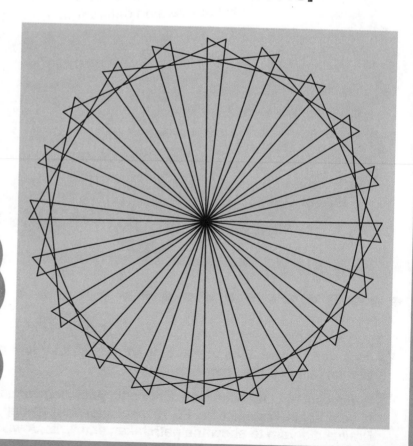

Activity 4

Try to produce this pattern with one line of instructions.

There are 20 triangles in this pattern.

Now try to be inventive and produce some more patterns.

REPETITION

Computers can be made to do clever things by giving them the right instructions. Better than that, they do not mind doing the same thing over and over without becoming bored. Also, they can repeat things very quickly and without making mistakes.

Making LOGO repeat some actions can save you work:

- You can make LOGO repeat something by using the word REPEAT.
- You also have to tell it what to repeat and how many times to repeat it.
- *The action you want to repeat goes inside square brackets.*
- *You can put lots of actions in the brackets.*
- When you use REPEAT, you are using what programmers call a <u>loop</u>.

Activity 1
Try this out.
REPEAT 4 [FD 100 RT 90]
What happened? Where did the turtle end up?

REGULAR SHAPES

In Activity 1, you turned the turtle through right angles to draw a square. A right angle is 90°. There are 4 sides to a square. If we didn't know that a right angle was 90°, we could work out the correct angle by dividing 360 (the number of degrees in a circle) by 4 to get 90. There is no need for us to do this when we can make the computer do it for us.

The command **REPEAT 4 [FD 100 RT 360/4]** draws a square again!

We can make any regular shape we want without any effort.

A pentagon has 5 sides. Here is how to make one.

REPEAT 5 [FD 100 RT 360/5]

Activity 2
Make a hexagon and a few other regular shapes. You may have to reduce the length of the sides to fit the screen.

OTHER REPEATING PATTERNS

All sorts of impressive patterns can be programmed with just a few repeating instructions.

Activity 3
What shape does this code produce?
REPEAT 40 [FD 100 BK 100 RT 360/40]
Try to adapt the code to draw a more or less solid circle.

REVIEW

5 As a class, list day-to-day activities that involve doing the same thing several times.

6 Work out what this will do. Draw what will happen.
PU LT 90 FD 200 RT 90 PD REPEAT 4 [REPEAT 4 [FD 50 RT 90] RT 90 PU FD 100 LT 90 PD]

PROCEDURES 1

AIMS

- **To see that storing commands in procedures has lots of advantages when writing programs**
- **To make things easier for ourselves by storing our instructions**
- **To make procedures that use other procedures**
- **To save our work**

STARTER

Operating systems make it easy to keep work tidy by letting us make <u>directories</u> or <u>folders</u> to keep things separate. Find out how to use your operating system to make a folder for your LOGO work.

⏺ Setting the scene

You have now programmed the computer to make patterns by using REPEAT instructions. Next, you will learn about how to make things easier by storing the instructions.

MAKING A PROCEDURE

We shall create two small procedures, and then put them together to make a third procedure that draws a simple house.

Activity 2

Activate your procedure builder and start a procedure called **SQUARE**.

> **Depending on your version of LOGO, you will probably need to type something like TO SQUARE**

Now, type in the commands we used earlier to make a square:
REPEAT 4 [FD 100 RT 90]
That's all we want in this procedure. Tell LOGO to finish.

> **You may have to type END or use some control key combination to finish.**

Test the procedure by typing **SQUARE**.
If it works OK, create another procedure called **TRIANGLE**. In that one, type
REPEAT 3 [FD 100 RT 120]
Clear the screen and test it.

Now, we make one more procedure to put it all together. Call it **HOUSE**. Enter these commands and store it.
SQUARE
FD 100
RT 30
TRIANGLE
Test the whole program by typing **HOUSE**.
Write another procedure called **STREET** to draw a row of houses like this.

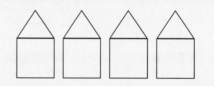

Find out how to save your work to make sure that you have these procedures for the future. Save them in the folder you created for your LOGO work.

WHAT ARE PROCEDURES?

We have given the computer instructions by typing in a list of commands.
It would be much easier if we could store these instructions.

Even better would be to store instructions in groups.

That way, we could re-use sets of instructions that were successful for us.

We can do all this by packaging groups of commands into <u>procedures</u>.

Advantages in using procedures
They make building a program much easier.
They save lots of work.
Once we have tested a procedure, we can use it again, knowing that it should work.

We can then build programs by grouping the procedures together.

How to write a procedure
Tell LOGO that you want a procedure.
Give it a name.
Type the commands.
When you have finished, tell LOGO to stop storing the commands.

We then run a procedure by typing its name.

If our procedure doesn't work properly, we call it back to edit it, and then try running it again.

Activity 1

In most versions of LOGO, the word 'TO' is used to make a procedure. Some versions use the word 'build' instead.
Find out how to do these things:
- Create a procedure in your version of LOGO.
- Tell LOGO that you have finished writing a procedure.
- Edit a procedure that you have previously created.

REVIEW

3 When you write instructions for a procedure like STREET, not everyone will have the same instructions in the same order, but will still have a street. As a class, spend 5 minutes discussing why.

4 Using ordinary simple words, write a set of procedures for a 'human computer' to make 6 slices of buttered toast.

PROCEDURES 2

AIMS
- To see how procedures can be made to behave differently each time we run them
- **To learn about variables and how they can be changed during a program**
- To make the procedures more useful and to test them

STARTER

Setting the scene
You have seen how procedures can make it easier to develop programs. In this lesson, you will learn about parameters – a way of making the procedures even more useful.

It is important that you keep your work safe so that you can access it later. If a computer has a problem, you may lose your work.

If you save work on the school network, someone will back it up (take a copy) from time to time. It is a good idea for you to keep copies of work as well.

● Find out how often your network is backed up and how it is done.

● Ask how you can make extra copies of your work to be really safe and so you can access it from home.

PARAMETERS

We have written some procedures to make building a program easier. We can do better than this and make procedures behave differently on different occasions.

For example, we may often want to make a square, but perhaps, next time, we shall need a different sized square.

We can make the procedure take account of our requirements by feeding it with a different number each time we use it. This number is called a <u>parameter</u>.

Activity 1
Start setting up a procedure. Name it as
TO SQUARE :SIDE

Putting the word SIDE in the procedure (after the colon) will let us change the size of the square's sides.

All that goes into the procedure is this:
REPEAT 4 [FD :SIDE RT 90]
Test this procedure by typing **SQUARE 100**
Then try **SQUARE 200**
A different-sized square is drawn according to the parameter you give to the procedure.

Square 30

Square 100

It is important that the parameter is included, and that it is correct.

Activity 2
Try typing these commands.
- □ **SQUARE**
- □ **SQUARE Z**
- □ **SQUARE 30 + 50**
What happens?

VARIABLES

When we tell the computer to use the word **SIDE**, we are, in fact, giving
ourselves even more opportunities to make things automatic.
We can change the value of **SIDE**
while the program is running.
SIDE is a <u>variable</u>.

Activity 3

Make another procedure called **LOTS**.
Make sure it can take a value
by including the word **:SIDE**.
Depending on your version of LOGO,
you will type something like this:
TO LOTS :SIDE
REPEAT 10 [SQUARE :SIDE MAKE SIDE :SIDE + 10]
END
What we are doing here is increasing
the value of **SIDE**
each time we repeat the square.
Test this by typing **LOTS 10**.
Now, write another procedure
to make this shape.

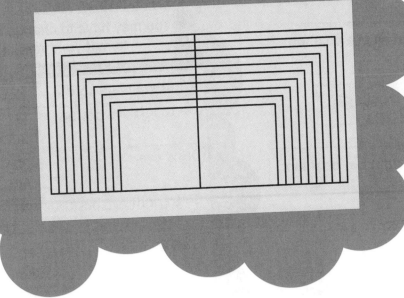

REVIEW

4 In pairs, write a procedure to make a rectangle. Then, as a class, spend 5 minutes
comparing the procedures you have written.

5 List the devices and appliances in your home that you can program.
In other words, list those that you can make behave in different ways
each time you use them.

FLOW CHARTS

AIMS
- **To look at how we can plan a project**
- To find positions on the screen
- **To plan what we want to do with a flow chart**
- To put a flow chart to work

STARTER

Spend 5 minutes looking at the **shortcuts** in your word processor. How can you find out what keys to press to perform a command quickly?

⚙ Setting the scene

You have now done a lot of work with procedures and built programs with them. In this lesson, you will start looking at how to plan a project, using a flow chart.

FLOW CHART

You can make your plans by writing a series of statements in boxes to make a simple flow chart.

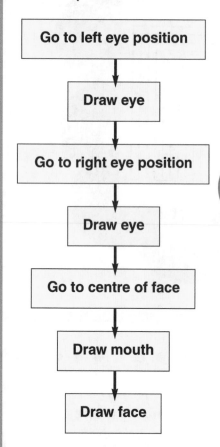

Go to left eye position

↓

Draw eye

↓

Go to right eye position

↓

Draw eye

↓

Go to centre of face

↓

Draw mouth

↓

Draw face

Activity 3

We shall use this flow chart to draw a face.

You may have to change some commands to suit your version of LOGO.

What we want to do	How we might do it
Go to left eye position	PU SETXY –50 50
Draw eye	PD ARC 360 10
Go to right eye position	PU SETXY 50 50
Draw eye	PD ARC 360 10
Go to centre of face	PU SETXY 0 0
Draw mouth	PD SETHEADING 90 ARC 180 50
Draw face	ARC 360 100

When you have these basic ideas, it will be easier to write the correct instructions.

SHORTCUTS

When you are writing programs, you will manage much better if you can type quickly and accurately. Try to avoid using the mouse if you can. The keyboard is quicker. There are lots of tricks with the keyboard that can save you work.

Follow the mouse:
http://www.noacsc.org/mercer/ce/CMtype.htm

Activity 1

Load your word processor and type a paragraph as quickly as you can. You can copy this paragraph if you want. Try to use all your fingers.
Now, try these key combinations:
- ☐ Ctrl-home (that means hold down the control key and then press home)
- ☐ Ctrl-end, shift-ctrl-home
- ☐ Shift-right arrow
- ☐ Shift-ctrl-right arrow.

Move text around by highlighting (use shift and arrow keys, not the mouse) and try Ctrl-x followed by Ctrl-v.
Find out what Ctrl-c does.

FINDING SCREEN POSITIONS

We shall now plan how to draw a smiley face using LOGO.
First we need to know where to put the parts.
We can use the command SETXY.

- ● X and Y are called co-ordinates.
- ● X is the distance across the screen from left to right.
- ● Y is the distance up and down the screen.

Always start with a plan. If you write instructions before you know where you are going, you can easily make mistakes.

Activity 2

In this activity, you will learn how to position the turtle anywhere you want on the screen.
On Worksheet 39, plot the point (0,0) in the middle.
Now key **CS**. Check that this puts the turtle in the centre of your screen. This has the same effect as **SETXY 0 0**.
Now key these **SETXY** commands. (Make sure you leave a space between the two numbers.)

SETXY 50 50
SETXY −50 50
SETXY −50 −50

See what happens and plot each point on Worksheet 39.
Key **CS** again to clear the screen. Then key **PU** (pen up).
Repeat the **SETXY** commands and see what effect this has.

REVIEW

4 As a class, produce a flow chart to show how to start working on your word processor.

5 Make a flow chart to describe the main steps needed either to make a cup of tea or to find your way to school.

TRAFFIC LIGHTS

AIMS

- To put flowcharting to use in a real-life situation
- To look at how a computer can be set to control things
- **To look at how instructions can be given to traffic lights**
- To see how a computer's output port can be set to control a device

STARTER

◐ *Setting the scene*

In this lesson, you will use a flow chart for a real-life situation: controlling traffic lights.

In small groups, make a list of electrical devices that you can find around the home, the school or anywhere else.

Divide them into 2 groups – those that always do the same thing and those that can be set to do different things according to what you want. The ones that can do different things are probably computer controlled.

As a class, look at each other's lists. Count how many of each type there are.

SEQUENCING TRAFFIC LIGHTS

One common situation that can be controlled by a computer is a set of traffic lights. It is important that the lights follow certain rules so that cars don't crash.

Activity 2 WS 40

Look at this diagram of a simple crossroads.
Traffic lights A work together (show the same lights)
and lights B work together.
Make a table to show the correct sequence of lights.
Use Worksheet 40 to help you.

INSTRUCTING THE LIGHTS

You can write a set of instructions to control the traffic lights just as you did when controlling the turtle in LOGO.
They could start as follows:

- *Switch green A off.*
- *Switch amber A on.*
- *Wait 5 seconds.*
- *Switch amber A off.*

- *Switch red A on.*
- *Switch green B off.*
- *Switch amber B on.*
- *etc.*

Activity 3

Complete the instructions to control the set of traffic lights.

CONTROLLING THINGS

More and more, computers are used to take control of things. They are used for lots of reasons:

- They don't get tired.
- They don't take a break.
- They don't go on strike.
- They don't need wages.
- They don't make mistakes.
- They don't complain.
- They don't become bored.

You could probably add to the list.

There are two main reasons though:

- Computers are very accurate.
- They can carry out the same instructions again and again in exactly the same way.

With computer technology, all sorts of devices can be programmed to do useful things and more importantly, they can be programmed differently on different occasions.

Activity 1

Choose 2 things that are controlled by a computer. Write a few sentences explaining how they behave differently on different occasions.

CONTROL

Activity 4

Use Worksheet 41 to help you. Fill in the state of the output ports for each stage of the traffic light sequence that you worked out in Activity 2.

Computers control things through an **output port**. Often, an output port has eight lines (wires) coming from it. These can be numbered 0–7. They are connected to the traffic lights like this. (Lines 3 and 4 are not used.)

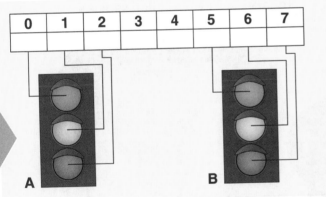

0	1	2	3	4	5	6	7

A   B

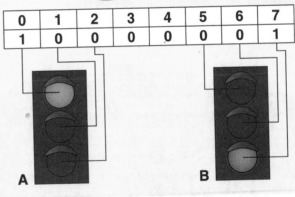

0	1	2	3	4	5	6	7
1	0	0	0	0	0	0	1

A   B

If a light is to be switched on, a signal is sent from the correct output line. You can represent a line that is switched ON by a 1. If it is OFF, it is 0.

REVIEW

5 Here are the answers to three questions:
- Output port
- Program
- Procedure

Spend 5 minutes thinking what the questions might be.
Then, as a class, spend 5 minutes comparing questions.

6 Suppose a computer has 4 lines in its output port and controls a washing machine.

0	1	2	3
Motor	Heater	Drain valve	Water supply valve

Draw the state of the output port as the machine goes through a simple wash/rinse cycle.

SENSORS

AIMS

* **To look at how computers know what is going on so they can control things**

STARTER

In small groups, make a list of household appliances that detect changes so they can work properly. For example, an electric iron stops heating up when it is the right temperature. Otherwise it may overheat.

As a group activity, put the lists together. Which appliances are mentioned the most?

⊕ Setting the scene

For computers to control things, they need to know what is going on around them. This lesson looks at how sensors are used to give information to a computer.

SENSORS

It is best if data is collected automatically. This allows it to be fed into the computer immediately. The computer can then respond immediately. This sort of computer system is called real-time.

There are lots of ways that data can be collected automatically. They all require the use of devices called <u>sensors</u>.

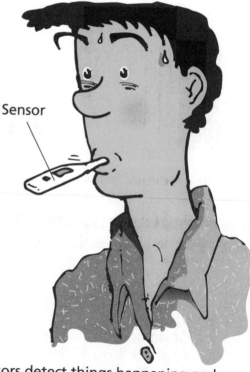

Sensor

Activity 3

Make a list of physical changes that might happen as traffic passes along the road. What sensors would be useful?

Sensors detect things happening and produce electrical signals that a computer can use. There are sensors that can detect almost anything such as heat, light, magnetic fields and sounds.

TRAFFIC LIGHT TIMING

Think back again to the traffic lights. We have looked at how to control them, by running through the sequence of light changes. Have you ever noticed that the time you wait at a particular red light is not always the same? The time on red may vary for all sorts of reasons.

Activity 1

Imagine that the local council has asked you to make recommendations about how long the red lights should be on at a particular crossroad. In small groups, write down what information you would need to collect so that you could make sensible suggestions.

GATHERING DATA

Activity 2

Think of some ways in which you could collect information about traffic flow in such a way that you can feed it into a computer-controlled traffic light system. Compare your ideas with others. Which do you think are the best ways and why?

Sometimes, traffic lights vary the time that they are on red according to how much traffic there is. It can be difficult to set the timing so that traffic keeps flowing as smoothly as possible. If a main road crosses a minor road, the main road will probably have a longer green phase than the minor one.

Maybe at certain times, there is more traffic in one direction than another. It can be useful to know how much traffic there is and then to adjust the timings to help the traffic flow.

REVIEW

4 Computer control is better if the computer knows what is going on. Sensors allow this to happen. There are sensors to detect most things.
When computers respond immediately to events, this is called <u>real-time processing</u>.
Think about the automatic doors in a shop. What activities need to be detected?
As a class, spend 5 minutes discussing what sensors are needed to make the doors operate safely.

5 List all the sensors you can think of around your home or in a car.
How do they help to control things?

PUTTING IT ALL TOGETHER

AIMS
- To see how inputs and outputs are needed to make a fully working computer control system
- To see how it is easiest to test a system by breaking it into small parts

STARTER

Setting the scene
This last lesson on control looks at how all the parts link together to make a control system.

By yourself, make a list of all the words you can think of that have something to do with computers controlling things.

Gather together your words with those that others have written down. Make sure that you know what they all mean.

FLOWCHARTING CONTROL PROCESS

A flow chart can be used to show how a control system works.

In this burglar alarm system, there are two sensors (the pressure pad and the infra-red detector) and one output device (the alarm).

If nothing happens to either of the sensors, the flow goes round again and again. This will continue until either one of them is activated or the alarm is switched off.

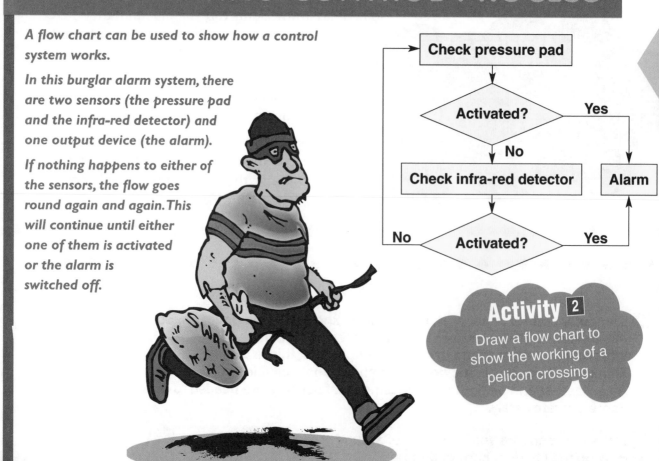

Check pressure pad

Activated? — Yes

No

Check infra-red detector — Alarm

No — Activated? — Yes

Activity 2
Draw a flow chart to show the working of a pelican crossing.

PROCESSING DATA

A computer system is made from a processor with other devices attached to it: from keyboards and mice to traffic lights and washing machine motors.

In each case, some of these devices send data to the processor. These are <u>input devices</u>. Other devices get data *from* the processor and send it out into the world, either for someone to look at or to make something happen. These are output devices.

Sometimes data is stored for the future.

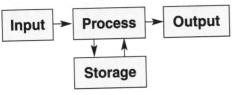

Activity 1

At a pelicon crossing, the traffic lights help pedestrians to cross the road.
Make a list of the input devices and output devices that are needed to make this work.
Which of these are sensors?

TESTING

All computer systems should be tested thoroughly. It is easy to make mistakes, especially when the computer system is complicated.

It is easiest to test it bit by bit. For example, in the burglar alarm system, we would need to test that the devices all work, but we also need to make sure that the software that controls it all also works.

We would probably have written a procedure for each part of the system. We would need at least three procedures:

- Check pressure pad
- Check infra red detector
- Sound alarm

Activity 3

Write down a testing procedure for the pelicon crossing system.

We would first need to make sure that each procedure works on its own. For example, we would input a signal to the procedure for *check pressure pad* and check that it produced an output.

We would do the same for the other sensor, and we would also check that an input into the *sound alarm* procedure produced an output signal.

We would eventually need to check that all the procedures work together.

REVIEW

4 As a class, spend 5 minutes comparing your answers to Activity 3.

5 Look back at any one of the LOGO tasks you did earlier. Make sure you have a copy of the commands. Explain how you could go about testing the whole project.

THE WEATHER PRESENTER

AIMS
- To look at the kind of data a weather presenter needs
- To see how computers can be used for collecting data

STARTER

As a class, spend about 5 minutes making a list of places where you could find information about the weather.

⊙⊙ Setting the scene

This unit is all about how computers are used by weather forecasters. In this first lesson, you will look at the kind of data the weather presenter needs.

COLLECTING WEATHER DATA

All sorts of data can be collected to help with weather forecasting. In the past, all this data was collected by hand, with people reading thermometers, pressure gauges and anemometers (for wind speed). This information was then passed on, often by telephone before being recorded manually. This took a lot of time!

Computers now help the process. They collect data automatically and store it. They then pass it on to other computers very quickly. This information can even be made available on the Internet.

Follow the mouse
http://www.metoffice.gov.uk/education/ukobs2.html

Activity 2
Search the Internet for details of the data collected from places in the UK during the last few hours. List the data collected.

WHY USE COMPUTERS?

Activity 3
Make a list of other advantages of using computers for this type of data collection.

Computers have lots of advantages when it comes to recording weather data:

- They can work 24 hours without a break.
- They are accurate.
- They can connect to sensors in places where people cannot live.

THE WEATHER CENTRE

Think about a typical weather forecast. The forecast says what type of weather might be expected in the next day or so.

To provide this information, the weather centre must first look at huge amounts of data. Then, the weather forecasters try to work out what might happen. The data comes from many places all over the country and the world. Satellite pictures also provide information.

Follow the mouse
www.bbc.co.uk
www.metoffice.gov.uk

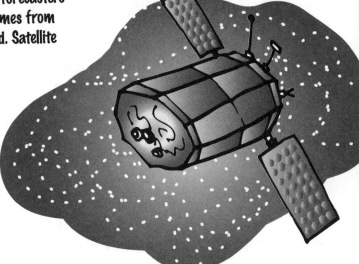

Activity 1

Visit some websites for weather information and look at today's weather forecast for your area on each site. Are they the same?

ANALOGUE AND DIGITAL DATA

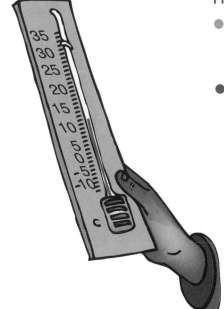

Physical data can be split into two types:

- **Analogue (continuous) data** changes gradually. The temperature in a room does not suddenly change from 15°C to 16°C. It changes steadily over a period of time.

- **Digital data** is two-state data, normally ON or OFF, YES or NO. There is no in between state.
  For example, 'Did it rain today?'.

Activity 4

Look at your list from Activity 2. Say which values are going to be continuous data and which, if any, are digital.

REVIEW

5 As a class, spend 5 minutes listing environmental changes that can be measured. Discuss how these changes might be measured.

6 Using newspapers, teletext or the Internet, make a table showing the temperatures in 5 different cities in Europe.

115

MEASURING WEATHER DATA

AIMS
- To look at how sensors measure the weather
- To find out how a weather station stores and records data

STARTER

Complete the activity on Worksheet 42. **WS 42**

◐◐ Setting the scene
In this lesson, you will discover how all the types of weather data can be collected.

A SCHOOL WEATHER STATION

This shows a typical school weather station.

The weather station collects data 24 hours a day and stores it in its own memory. A computer connected to the station is used to download and display the data.

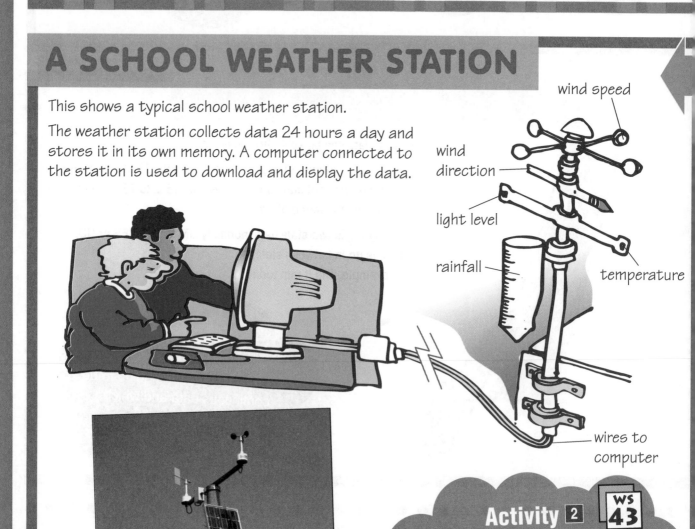

wind speed

wind direction

light level

rainfall

temperature

wires to computer

Activity 2 **WS 43**
Look at the diagram above and the data on Worksheet 43. For each item of data, write down which sensor would record that data.

COLLECTING DATA AUTOMATICALLY

We use _sensors_ to collect data automatically. Sensors are input devices that convert measurements into electrical signals. There are two types:

● _Analogue sensors_ measure a range of values for continuous data.

● _Digital sensors_ detect on or off values like a button being pressed.

The sensors are connected to a computer so that the data can be stored and saved automatically.

Activity 1

Make a list of any environmental data that you think can be measured by a computer using sensors.

SETTING THINGS UP

Activity 3

The best place for the weather station is on a roof top. Write some reasons for this.

The sensors on the weather station simply collect data. They do not process it. The data they collect is then made into information by the computer software. The computer is programmed to process the data in a certain way.

If the data is to be turned into information correctly then the weather station must be set up and tested.

For example, the light sensor points towards the east. It measures sunrise by detecting the light level. This means the weather station is set up facing the right direction.

WORKING WITH THE DATA

Here is a display showing some information from the weather station. The software is set up to show the information graphically.

Activity 4

Look at the screen for the weather station and answer these questions.

☐ What is the direction of the wind?
☐ How much rain has there been?
☐ How many hours of sunshine?
☐ What has been the highest temperature?

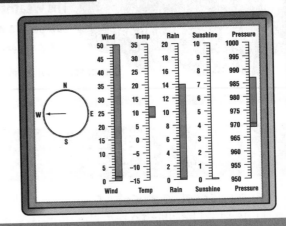

REVIEW

5 In pairs, list points to be considered when setting up a weather station.

6 As a class, spend 5 minutes sharing your ideas.

7 Using the information about the weather station from today's lesson, write a set of instructions for setting up a simple weather station like the one in the diagram.

PROCESSING STORED DATA

AIMS
- To look at data and information
- To use graphs and charts
- To import data into a spreadsheet
- To process weather data

STARTER

In pairs, spend about 5 minutes on Worksheet 44.

As a class, spend about 5 minutes comparing your ideas.

∞ Setting the scene
In this lesson, you will look at how weather data is processed. Next lesson, you will see what data logging is all about.

USING THE NUMBERS

Activity
2 Make a list of other things computers can do with data.

Computers process numbers very quickly and accurately. This means that very large sets of data can be processed very quickly.

The weather forecast is based on very large sets of data. Using computers means that this data can be processed very quickly to give better forecasts.

Computers can quickly calculate averages, calculate totals and put data into order.

IMPORTING DATA

Activity 3
Import Database 2 into your spreadsheet. Your teacher will tell you where to find the data.

A spreadsheet is a useful tool for handling numbers, but you need to be able to put the numbers into the spreadsheet first. Fortunately, a spreadsheet can take in numbers that have been collected using different software. When software takes in data that has been prepared by a different piece of software, this is called **importing** data.

Importing data needs the numbers to be in a standard form. One standard way of doing this is called CSV format. This means __comma separated variables__. In other words, the numbers are saved one after the other with commas in between like this.

26, 27, 25, 26, 22, 24

DATA AND INFORMATION

When the computer collects the data, it stores it as numbers on a disk. On their own, the numbers do not mean anything. To make the numbers into information you need to give them meaning in some way.

INFORMATION = DATA + MEANING

For example, 26092003 is a number but what does it mean?

● Is it telephone number?
● Is it the answer to a calculation?
● Is it an electricity meter reading?

It could really be anything but if you write it down as 26/09/2003 it is a date. Simple when you know how!

Activity 1

In pairs, spend about 5 minutes making up some data like the one in the example. Your partner can then try to guess how to make it into information.

GRAPHS AND CHARTS

Graphs can be very good ways of displaying information. The problem is that they can take a long time to draw by hand. The computer saves time by drawing the graph for you. This gives you more time to work out what it means.

Also, if you produce a graph with a computer and then do not like its layout or style, you can make changes very quickly.

Activity 4

Using the rainfall data you imported in Activity 3, produce a bar chart like this.

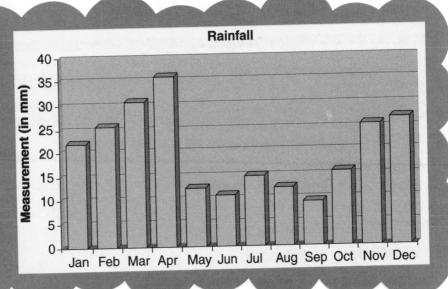

REVIEW

5 As a class, look at Worksheet 44 again. In what ways could a spreadsheet help with processing the data?

6 List the advantages and disadvantages of using computers to record and store data.

DATA LOGGING

AIMS
- To look at data logging
- **To learn about logging intervals and logging periods**

STARTER

Summers in the UK are getting wetter.

As a class, discuss how you could collect the evidence to prove – or disprove – this statement.

⊂⊃ Setting the scene

You have examined ways that we can process data. In this lesson, you will look at data logging. Then, in the next lesson, you shall look at interpreting and analysing data.

WHAT IS DATA LOGGING?

Data logging is capturing (collecting) data with sensors, storing it, and then making use of it later.

The sensors capture the data, which is saved. A computer can then be used to analyse the data and turn it into useful information.

Activity 1
Make a list of environmental data that you think could usefully be collected by a data logging system.

DATA LOGGING REQUIREMENTS

Data logging looks like a good idea, but you need some equipment!

- The right kind of sensors
- Some software to be able to use the sensors
- A computer to process the data
- Somewhere to store the data

Activity 3
Think of some tasks you could use data logging for and write down what the logging period and interval might be.

You also need to make some decisions:

- How long you are going to collect the data for – the logging period
- How long to wait between measurements – the logging interval

It is important for both of these to be right.

- If the logging period is too long, you waste time and collect too much data.
- If it is too short, you might not see the changes.

Normally, if the logging period is a long one, the logging interval can be long as well.

For example, to measure the change in temperature of a room over a day, a reading once an hour will be enough. However, to measure the change in temperature as an ice cube melts during one hour, a reading every 30 seconds might be a good idea.

REASONS FOR DATA LOGGING

You already know some of the reasons for using a computer for analysing data.

Here are some examples of situations where you might want to use data logging to collect data:

- Data is needed over a very long period of time.
- The data is produced very rapidly.
- The data is produced in a dangerous place, such as inside the reactor of a nuclear power station or an oven in a bakery.
- The data is collected from a place where humans cannot easily go, such as space or in narrow tunnels.

Activity 2

Look at the list in this panel. Write down why you think using data logging and a computer is useful in each case.

REVIEW

4 As a class, spend 5 minutes making a complete list from your answers to Activity 3.

5 A friend of yours thinks that his bedroom is too cold and wants to collect some data to show his parents. Write some notes telling your friend how data logging might help.

INTERPRETING DATA

AIMS
- To look at how the data that is logged needs to be interpreted
- To look at how the weather data is used

STARTER

Complete Worksheet 45.

WS 45

⚮ *Setting the scene*

Logged data needs to be interpreted. In this lesson, you will look at how to process the data.

INTERPRETING DATA

The temperature data still means very little - all that can be seen is that the temperature changed. But what does it mean?

To work this out, it is important to know where and how the data was collected. Then, the data can be interpreted more clearly.

Remember: INFORMATION = DATA + MEANING.

Amy carried a data-logging device from the science lab in one part of the school to the computer room in another part of the school.

To reach the computer room, she needed to go outside.

Does the data make more sense now?

Activity 2

Look at the data again and answer these questions:

- ☐ Which room was the warmest?
- ☐ For how long was Amy outside?
- ☐ What was the temperature outside?
- ☐ How long was she in the computer room before the device stopped logging?

BACK TO THE WEATHER

We have already seen that a weather forecaster requires lots of collected data. But how is it used?

Forecasting the weather needs a lot of skill as well as a lot of data. The weather forecaster looks at the data from many readings collected together:

- Wind speed
- Wind direction
- Air pressure

Activity 3

WS 46

Complete Worksheet 46.

Follow the mouse
http://www.metoffice.gov.uk/education/curriculum/leaflets/weathermaps.html

DATA ANALYSIS

Data logging can collect lots of numbers, but numbers on their own might not reveal much. The data that is collected needs to be carefully analysed to see what is happening. There are many ways to do this:

- Sort the data into order.
- Find the average.
- Plot and interpret a graph.

Look at these figures.

Time (minutes)	Temperature (degrees C)
1	20
2	20
3	12
4	12
5	21
6	21
7	21

Activity 1

Describe in your own words what the data shows.
What was the logging period?
What was the logging interval?

Now, look at this graph.

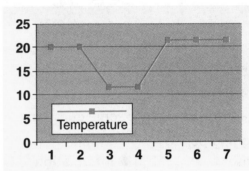

Which is easier to follow?

HAVE A GO!

Look at this graph.
Amy has been walking about the school again with a data-logging device. The data-logging device has 3 sensors.

Light sensor	The higher the number, the more light
Temperature sensor	Degrees Celsius
Sound sensor	The higher the number, the greater the noise

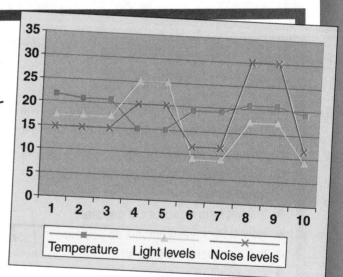

She has been in 3 places:

- A long corridor with very few windows
- A classroom just before the teacher arrives
- The computer room where everyone is working hard

Activity 4

On Worksheet 47, mark where you think Amy is. WS 47

REVIEW

5 As a class, spend 5 minutes discussing how you have interpreted the data in Activity 4.

6 Using your graph from Activity 4, write out an explanation for your answers.

DATA LOGGING EXPERIMENT

AIMS
- **To look at types of sensors**
- **To plan a data logging experiment**

STARTER

Here are the answers to some questions:

- Logging period
- Sensor
- Graph
- Information

In pairs, spend about 5 minutes writing some questions to go with these answers.

Then, as a class, spend about 5 minutes comparing your questions.

⚭ Setting the scene

In this final lesson of this unit, you will use your knowledge to design a datalogging experiment.

PLANNING

Before you write about your experiment, you will need to do some planning. Here are some of the things to think about:

- How many different things are you measuring?
- How long will the experiment last – minutes, hours, days?
- In what form do you want the data?
- How many measurements do you need?
- Is it a sequence of events?
- Is it a one-off event?
- How often do the measurements need to be taken?

Activity 3

Suppose you want to see how long it takes for a cup of coffee to go cold. Answer the questions listed on the left for this task.

Logging period is how long the experiment lasts

 START STOP

Logging interval is the time between readings

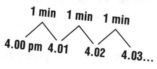
1 min   1 min   1 min
4.00 pm   4.01   4.02   4.03…

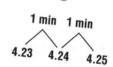
1 min   1 min
4.23   4.24   4.25